"You can't just read it once. Its truths grab hold of your being, force you to wrestle with reality, and only loosen their grasp on your soul when you begin to embrace the spiritual gifts of administration. Challenging and comforting, this book made me think, forced me to be honest, and enticed me into dialogue with others."

Leland Nagel
Executive Director
National Conference for Catechetical Leadership

"A cornucopia of refreshment for administrators' worried minds and weary spirits. Offering keen insights, holy companions, stories, and prayers, *Redeeming Administration* reclaims our work as vocation and rekindles our hearts to serve with joy!"

Celeste Mueller
Vice President
Formation and Theological Education
Ascension Health

"Our Catholic institutions are signs of Christ's saving mission. But they can only realize this sacramentality if they have administrators who see their work as holy. Garrido brings her considerable theological insight to bear on the administrator's vocation. She teaches us how to redeem our ministry and how to make even our most mundane work redemptive."

Rev. Charles E. Bouchard, O.P.
Prior Provincial
Dominican Province of St. Albert the Great

"I have found here a new required text! I deeply appreciate Garrido's earthy, humorous, and reflective style. She understands the challenges and gifts of administration, yet invites me to reflect differently about mundane tasks. For the first time, I can actually see my life in administration as the fruitful living out of a vocation of discipleship. I find her thinking, her turns of phrase, her deep scripture-and tradition-based reflections life changing."

Sharon Callahan
Associate Dean for Academic Programs and Student Life
School of Theology and Ministry
Seattle University

"This little book is a great pocket guide to nudge pastoral leaders and other Catholic administrators toward in-depth critical reflection, discernment, and leadership praxis that will make a profound difference in our twenty-first century Church."

Sr. Angela Ann Zuchowski, M.H.S.H.
Institute for Pastoral Initiatives Director
University of Dayton

"Garrido's book is a welcome resource for all those in ministry who find themselves thrust into administration. She shows how the work need not be draining but instead can become 'A spiritual pathway by which good people can become better. 'A delightful read for any Catholic leader!"

Brian Schmisek
Institute for Pastoral Studies Director
Loyola University Chicago

"A great help for those who tackle the great and small tasks of building God's reign through the work of administration. Garrido masterfully unites the experience of talented administrators with the wisdom and tradition of the Church to unveil the presence of God. She offers wonderful advice and tells the stories of exemplary saint-companions with humor and honesty. I highly recommend this book to anyone who works in administration in the Church!"

Kristen Hempstead McGann
Associate Director
Office for Catechesis and Youth Ministry
Archdiocese of Chicago

redeeming ADMINISTRATION

12 Spiritual Habits for Catholic Leaders
in Parishes, Schools, Religious Communities, and Other Institutions

Ann M. Garrido

Foreword by Gerard J. Olinger, C.S.C.

Ave Maria Press AVE Notre Dame, Indiana

Founded in 1865, Ave Maria Press is a ministry of the United States Province of Holy Cross.

www.avemariapress.com

Paperback: ISBN-10 1-59471-428-2 ISBN-13 978-1-59471-428-3

E-book: ISBN-10 1-59471-429-0 ISBN-13 978-1-59471-429-0

Cover image © istockphoto.com

Cover design by Kristen Hornyak Bonelli.

Text design by Katherine Robinson.

Printed and bound in the United States of America.

Library of Congress Cataloging-in-Publication Data is available.

This book is dedicated to

Diane Kennedy, O.P.,

who reminds me time and again,

"The ministry is in the interruption."

Contents

Foreword by Gerard J. Olinger, C.S.C. ~ ix

Preface ~ xi

Introduction ~ 1

Administration calls us to. . .

1. Breadth of Vision ~ 13
   Companion for the Journey: Angela Merici
2. Generativity ~ 27
   Companion for the Journey: Jordan of Saxony
3. Trust ~ 41
   Companion for the Journey: Louise de Marillac
4. Agape ~ 55
   Companion for the Journey: Richard of Chichester
5. Integrity ~ 67
   Companion for the Journey: Bruno
6. Humility ~ 81
   Companion for the Journey: Martha
7. Courage ~ 93
   Companion for the Journey: Ambrose
8. Reflection ~ 107
   Companion for the Journey: Joseph Mukasa Balikuddembe
9. Humor ~ 121
   Companion for the Journey: Thomas More

10. Forgiveness ~ 137

Companion for the Journey: Mary MacKillop

11. Embrace Death ~ 153

Companion for the Journey: Rose Philippine Duchesne

12. Hope ~ 169

Companion for the Journey: Gregory the Great

Administration Calls Us to Too Much ~ 187

Conclusion ~ 201

Foreword

As both a Holy Cross priest and vice president for student affairs at the University of Portland, I understand and share the struggle many have between being trained for ministry and being charged with administration. There are days when I am buried in email, meetings, budgets, and personnel decisions and I think to myself, "This is not why I wanted to become a Catholic priest!"

Ann Garrido's work on the spirituality of administration addresses this longing in my heart. In *Redeeming Administration,* she takes apart the false dichotomy that many sense between administration and ministry. She asks those of us who are administrators to reflect instead on how God is transforming us through the very work of administration into the people God "dreams us to be." Ann challenges "the poor reputation of administration as something that drains the light and life out of good people" and she reconceives it as "a potential spiritual pathway by which good people can become better people." Instead of looking at our work as pulling us away from the relationships and interactions that we often see as the real substance of ministry, Ann reminds administrators to focus on the ways that our work is truly a self-gift—a service to others. In this way, we follow Christ who pours out His life for others.

In addition to laying out twelve spiritual habits for administrators, Ann gives an example of a saint who embodies each of the virtues that she explores. She reminds us that we are not alone in the work that we do. United to others through administration, as well as to these companions from our Catholic tradition, we realize that we do not walk this road alone. Others have walked this path before us and provide footsteps for us to follow in. Some of the saints will be familiar to readers, while others will be new, illustrating the way that administration has been seen as a ministry from the time of St. Paul's writings and throughout the history of the Church.

Redeeming Administration has provided me with a new way of seeing my role in the Catholic institution that I serve and a new understanding that it is a true ministry, a crucial work in the kingdom of God. Organizations need pastoral care every bit as much as individuals, and a good administrator, like a good pastor, must listen carefully. Anyone charged with an administrative position in a Catholic setting who is looking to find spiritual meaning in their day-to-day work—and I know there are many who are—will benefit from the rich theological and pastoral insights in this thought-provoking and warmly inspiring book. Here is an excellent contribution to the life of the Church!

In Holy Cross,

Rev. Gerard J. Olinger, C.S.C.

Vice President for Student Affairs, University of Portland

Preface

This slender volume took about six years of consistent effort for me to write. It is not that the prose is particularly dense or profound. It is not that I struggled with language or coming up with material. And it is not for lack of support or interest—indeed my colleagues at work and my family at home have been nothing but encouraging. No, the problem—as you may have guessed—is that I am an administrator.

My day job is working as a program director at a small graduate school of theology in the Midwest. And so my typical day goes somewhat like this: I sit down at the desk in the morning with a cup of tea, determined to spend some time with the project at hand. I turn on my computer; I decide to check e-mail first. Four hours later, I realize I haven't written a page yet and open up my document and become aware that I have a meeting in five more minutes and haven't made it to the restroom since drinking that cup of tea. I return from the meeting with an agenda of items that need urgent attention, and a student walks in to chat. My telephone rings; mail arrives; then I'm off to another meeting. Now it is time to go home. I look at the document opened in the morning and find it is still blank, perhaps with a random phone number typed onto it. I can't quite remember to whom the number belongs and whether or not I was supposed to call the person back.

The problem is not that I am a poor administrator with no propensity for the work. Indeed, I think signs of this vocation have been present since childhood. Not long ago I discovered a series of notebooks in my parents' attic that were filled with—I kid you not—page after page of curricular charts for a congregation, which I had founded in my imagination, of six thousand sisters who needed training for the numerous ministries in which I had imagined they would be involved. As I ruffled through the pages, my mother pulled out a monastery I had created from cardboard shoeboxes. My primary joy had been designing a schedule for what the tiny clay nuns would do at various points in their day—sometimes down to three-minute intervals—and then moving them accordingly. Please don't laugh. Some of us just can't help wanting to add a little order to the world.

But this doesn't mean that administration is something that comes easily to me, or that I find it particularly enlivening or satisfying. Many days it is just the opposite. I find it draining, occasionally even boring—filled with detailed tasks that rob me of "the big thought" I long to have. It fractures my day into tiny shards of time that make it impossible to concentrate or get anything of substance accomplished. It wakes me up in the middle of the night with haunting thoughts of something I have forgotten to do (indeed, it is four in the morning as I type these words). And I'm certain that it contributes to my need to buy in bulk Excedrin Migraine).

These are the experiences that led me to work on this book in the first place. It was just about six years ago that I realized that I must either uncover some way of finding meaning in my job or I must quit. And, as you can see, I am still here.

Introduction

In Paul's first letter to the Corinthians, administrators make a rare scriptural appearance:

> Now you are Christ's body, and individually parts of it. Some people God has designated in the church to be, first, apostles; second, prophets; third, teachers; then, mighty deeds; then, gifts of healing, assistance, administration, and varieties of tongues. Are all apostles? Are all prophets? Are all teachers? Do all work mighty deeds? Do all have gifts of healing? Do all speak in tongues? Do all interpret? Strive eagerly for the greatest spiritual gifts. (1 Cor 12:27–31a)

It is one of Paul's most eloquent and meaningful passages concerning the multiplicity of gifts that work together in the Church toward a common mission, and yet it is somewhat humorous from an administrator's point of view. In Corinthians, Paul is arguing against a hierarchy of ministries in which some members of the community are considered more valuable than others, yet one cannot help but notice administrators fall toward the end of Paul's list, just before those who speak in tongues. When Paul, with rhetorical flourish, begins to relist each of the gifts in the second half of the passage to emphasize his point, administration somehow slips away and does not reappear.

In history, the Church has often persisted in Paul's forgetfulness, acknowledging administration as a gift needed for the life of the community, but not giving extensive consideration as to how. The divinity library that I frequent is a marvelous, four-story building with entire shelves devoted to preaching, teaching, and healing and how each is a way of living out one's discipleship in Christ—a path toward holiness. Yet, the administration section of this library reveals very slim pickings.

Administration in ecclesial life has often been distained by both those who work within the ministry and those who do not. Within the ministry, administrative tasks are often considered odious, taking us away from what drew us into ministry in the first place: teaching, serving the poor, being at the bedside, "hanging" with the teens. From the perspective of those outside the ministry, administration is frequently viewed as an oppressive force, spoken about in hushed tones of suspicion around the coffeemaker. Both those called to the ministry of administration and those who are not look upon the role with reservation, as if close contact might result in spiritual tainting of some sort.

Such fears are not unfounded. All of us can cite administrators who seemed to become less personable, less human in the role. We can name men and women who once were regarded as creative, vivacious, and understanding people until they became administrators—and now they are exceedingly difficult to live alongside. "He was a great priest," we will comment, "but you hardly recognize him anymore since he's become vicar general." "She used to be so fun to be around," we will lament. "Now she only obsesses about the budget and appearances." I have heard similar comments surface at my family dinner table in reference to me. There are times when administrative work has made me less the person I want to be.

When I was a child, the Act of Contrition I was taught to recite included the promise to avoid, not only sin, but also "all near occasions of sin." From very early in life, we were instructed to stay away from situations that would tempt us. Administration, it would seem, clearly fits this bill since it always places a person in a role of some power, increasing the possibility that one might misuse and abuse this power. Administration generally requires a person to steward money and resources—increasing opportunities to serve one's own interests. And, furthermore, administration requires the continual exercise of judgment, a faculty about which

Jesus sowed suspicion, saying that it belonged only to God.

There is wisdom in the admonition to avoid temptation. On the other hand, near occasions of sin can also become occasions in which virtue can be practiced and honed in a quite intentional way. Near occasions of sin force us to take a stand, to make decisions, to define ourselves. In short, it is in the near occasions of sin that we can also become saints.

There is a bit of a mystery here. All professional ministry—including administrative ministry—is a one-directional activity: we are not in it for ourselves but for the other. We cannot expect those we serve to meet our needs. Yet, in the mysterious graciousness of God, we often find that our work with others does feed us at a very deep level. In the doing of ministry, God places before us the people and situations we most need to encounter, moving us along our own spiritual journey.

In this book, I want to challenge the poor reputation of administration as something that drains the light and life out of good people and reconceive it as a potential spiritual pathway by which good people can become better people—people distinguished by a certain translucence and aliveness that extend beyond themselves and into the institutions they serve. In theological language, I want to argue that administration can be a praxis—an activity that has the potential to transform, not only the lives of others, but also an administrator's own life and way of being in the world. I hope to redeem administration by exploring twelve habits that together form the spiritual fabric of this most vital ministry of Christ's Church.

So, what do we mean by a spirituality of administration? In order to answer that question, it might be helpful if I first define what I mean by administration. Most dictionary definitions are remarkably unhelpful, referring to administration simply as "the act or process of administering." Clearly "administer" shares a common root with the word "ministry" and therefore a common understanding of service to others. It bears the Latin prefix ad, meaning "to" or "toward." For the sake of this book, we might think of administration as activities that move *toward* ministry or service, activities that enable ministry or service to take place. Administering usually implies the organization and oversight of programs and personnel for the larger mission of an institution. It involves activities such as attending committee meetings, organizing agendas and preparing meeting minutes, managing budgets and employees, and maintaining an office environment. It includes responding to phone calls and e-mail, while sorting out what can be ignored and what needs to be delegated or shared with others. The list, of course, does not end there, but it gives you a sense of the kind of work to which I am referring.

How is administering different than leading? Obviously the two overlap significantly. The difference for me is a question of nuance. Leadership tilts toward the creation of vision and policy, sometimes within an institution, sometimes not. Administration tilts toward the execution and management of vision and policy, almost always within an institution. Obviously leadership benefits from some organizational skills and administration benefits from a visionary spirit, so rigid boundaries between the two need not be drawn. In this book, though, I will be focusing more on the execution and management aspects of our work. I recognize that, for some, administration comprises the entirety of their position; for others, administration is just one component of a leadership or other ministerial role.

Perhaps more important to our task than a definition of administration, however, is answering the question, "What is spirituality?" Much has been written in recent years about spirituality, in religious circles and beyond. A significant portion of this literature implies that the life of the spirit is separate from daily life, with its traffic and meetings and clogged plumbing in the first-floor bathroom. It focuses on that part of the day, week, or year that we can dedicate to silence, to being "away from it all," to stepping out of the chaos and morass of our routine existence. And yet, while time for silence and retreat is very valuable and necessary, at the heart of the Catholic sacramental tradition lays the conviction that God loves the world. God chooses to make God's very self known to us through created matter—the matter of bread and wine, water and oil—but also in the created matter of our particular lives—our families, work, parishes, schools, neighborhoods, and congregations.

While there are many conceivable ways of defining spirituality, one possibility is simply to say that spirituality is the particular way in which God works out our salvation in this world. It is, in essence, the particular way in which God brings us into the fullness of life and light for which we are intended. So, if we speak of a Christian spirituality, we mean that Jesus Christ plays an integral and central role in our salvation. Or, if we speak of a marital spirituality, we mean that it is through the experience of being married that God intends to make us into the people we are meant to be. If we speak of a ministerial spirituality, we pause to reflect on how, through the practice of ministry, God is transforming the minister. And hence, when we speak of the spirituality of administration, the key question we will want to ask is, "How is the ministry of administration somehow part of the way that God is transforming me into the person God dreams me to be?"

In the Judeo-Christian tradition, to receive a vocation or a call from God is frequently an invitation to movement. In Genesis, we find the first words that God ever speaks to our father in faith Abraham: "Come out!" (Gn 12:1). In the Gospel of John, we find Jesus' words about the work of the Good Shepherd who "calls his own by name and leads them out" (Jn 10:3). Calls impel us "out" of ourselves to something more, something beyond. As Margaret, a character in Gail Godwin's novel *Evensong*, points out, "Something is your vocation if it keeps making more of you."

My own experience in administration has borne out this truth. I have come to discern a call to administration in part because administration has continually called me to "come out" of myself, "come out" of my comfort zone, so that I can become something *more*. Unlike other jobs I've held that afforded some sense of real competence, administration has been a place of continued challenge, always stretching me to grow. Even when I thought I was done with it, it was never done with me.

Each administrator's journey is unique and particular. Yet, when we think about the *more* that administration wants to make of us, I hypothesize that there are several key virtues, dispositions, or spiritual habits that the ministry consistently cultivates. This is not to say that we will become holier people simply by sitting at the desk and staring at a computer screen long enough. There is always an element of choice involved! But it *is* to say that if we are attentive to the potential grace present in the day-to-day responsibilities we tackle as administrators, we can be formed and molded in profound ways. The key is to be aware of and open to the invitation each day at the desk presents. I truly am not trying to add things to your schedule; I am sure it is already very full. I am not suggesting increased time for prayer or a retreat, welcome though these might be. Rather, I want to highlight the spiritual possibilities in what you are *already* doing.

In this book, I reflect on twelve potential fruits of administration that I have experienced blossoming in my life and in the lives of fellow administrators I have come to admire. Alongside each of these fruits or spiritual habits, I've identified a holy administrator from our Church's calendar whose life exemplifies the particular fruit discussed. As noted before, popular lore provides few models for the particular spiritual road that we trod. The men and women featured here let us know that we do not walk alone. We discover others, across generations, have pursued holiness in the context of administration. Some of these persons will likely be new friends. Some will be familiar to you, but perhaps you have not considered them before through the lens of administration.

Like you and me, none of these administrators functioned in ideal situations. But in the reality that was their lot, they did the best they were able—lending their giftedness and goodwill to the grace of the role. Sometimes their efforts on behalf of the Church were successful; many times they failed. But whether or not their work produced the desired effects in their settings or within their institutions, it certainly had a lasting effect on both the places in which they ministered and on the persons God intended each of them to be. They model administration as a praxis—an avenue for self-transformation.

Why twelve habits and twelve administrators? The inspiration comes from a passage in the closing chapter of Revelation: "On either side of the river is the tree of life with its twelve kinds of fruit, producing its fruit each month; and the leaves of the tree are for the healing of the nations" (Rv 22:2 NRSV). I have come to think of administration, for better or for worse, as the tree of life in which I live. I can see it is a very fertile tree that bears not only fruit or rich spiritual habits year-round but also different kinds of fruit in different kinds of seasons. And it is a tree that is ultimately intended, not for itself, but for the larger purposes of God, for "the healing of the nations." Choosing twelve habits reminds me to think of my work as a place of abundance and fecundity.

Clearly, the number twelve also lends itself nicely to reading this book over the course of a year—perhaps alone, perhaps with a group of fellow administrators—with one fruit for each month. I thoroughly encourage this approach. We are administrators. We are very busy people. We get lots of our nourishment by nibbling while on the go. So feel free to read and digest this book in small bites, hopefully picking up one good habit at a time.

Administration calls us to . . .

1. Breadth of Vision

Every day, human interdependence grows more tightly drawn and spreads by degrees over the whole world. . . . Every social group must take account of the needs and legitimate aspirations of other groups, and even of the general welfare of the entire human family.

—Second Vatican Council
Gaudium et Spes, 26

Some jobs invite us to do one thing and do it well. We are only responsible for our own piece of the puzzle and need not worry about the rest. That is someone else's job. We don't often know who that someone else is that takes care of the rest; we only know that it should be done. That it *needs* to be done. What many fail to realize is that the mysterious someone else stitching together the spaces left between all the other jobs is usually the administrator.

Administrators, like kids, come to know the darnedest things. They know the number of the copy-machine repair company and where the paper clips are kept. They know who will be out of the office on vacation in April and how this will affect the launch date for the new program. They know that the IT department can't move on the installation of updated software as scheduled, because an invalid budget code submitted last month has delayed the process. And they know that the plunger is in the janitor's closet on the third floor, on the right side of the mop.

Administrators possess, more than most, a vision of the whole of an organization—an understanding of how all of the parts fit together and work in relation to one another. Rather than being able to see only from one department's viewpoint, they grasp the interplay of all perspectives, and appreciate how they harmonize or compete. They see how the action of one might impact the others. In this way, administration stretches the intellectual capacities of those who hold positions in this field—helping them to illumine dynamics between the components of institutional life that others would miss.

More important, administration can cultivate spiritual growth—expanding not just one's mind but also one's heart, to love and desire the common good, the flourishing of all. The breadth of vision that administration fosters can lead to a wideness of spirit—magnanimity—in which administrators learn to sublimate even their own agendas and aspirations to what would best serve the good of the whole. They are moved beyond pettiness and fixation on the details toward the big picture. Aristotle considered magnanimity the crowning virtue in his hierarchy of virtues.

To the degree that administrators are able to hold and carry the big picture of an organization, they participate somehow in the mystery of God, who holds and carries the biggest picture of all. They share in something of God's grand vision and spirit and experience something of how God sees and loves our universe. Administrators become, like the prophets of the Hebrew scriptures, "friends of God"—persons who are able to empathize with the challenges God faces in a most particular way and therefore serve as good counsel. They understand better than most why things are the way they are and know there is always more to the story than what nearly everyone thinks. They sympathize with the plight of the Creator to answer for the current state of the planet and to deal with the innumerable requests from every nation on earth to uphold its specific agenda. In return, administrators draw inspiration, consolation, and guidance from a

God who sees and loves the whole from the dawn of creation.

When I consider God as the Divine Administrator, the scripture verses that most come to mind are from the opening chapters of Genesis. I have always found it fascinating that Genesis includes two narratives of the earth's creation. The first one (Gn 1:1–2:3) describes creation as a very well-organized event. In due order, light is separated from darkness, then the water from the dry land. Plants arrive, then animals. God carefully prepares the world step-by-step for the arrival of humanity, so that when the first humans come onto the scene on the sixth day, everything they need and more has already been put into place. The second account (Gn 2:4–25) paints a very different picture: God creates the human first and then suddenly realizes, "Oh, this guy is going to need someplace to live!" After fashioning a garden and many animal companions, God wakes up to the fact, "This isn't quite working; my human creature is lonely!" And the being that was once one becomes two.

I often fancy myself imaging God from the first story—carefully unrolling my new program in an orderly, step-by-step process in which everything proceeds smoothly. In reality, my administration often looks far more like the second account: "Oh, welcome to the staff! Now, I bet you are going to need an office! And, oh yes, a telephone!"

From whichever account we draw our inspiration, counsel, and guidance, however, we recognize that what both share in common is a Creator who takes great care to establish an environment in which life can blossom. God's primary work is to set a stage, give a space, and create the conditions in which a diversity of creatures can flourish. The God of Genesis is intimately involved in this space. Indeed, in the second account, God enjoys personally walking through the garden. But one doesn't get the sense that God is micromanaging here; God has created a place where humans are free to roam and discover with very few prohibitions. When humanity violates the one great prohibition, God does not step in and try to fix everything. God sews the humans some clothes—again, remaining intimately involved with them—but leaves them to work out the consequences of their actions.

Likewise, I have come to understand that the primary task of the administrator involves the creation of an environment in which life can flourish. It has to do with establishing and maintaining the kind of order necessary for human freedom and creativity to function unimpeded. It sounds very simplistic, but if the copy machine is working and the stapler has staples, if people know where to turn when they have a concern and can find out the protocol for addressing a conflict, then the organization becomes the kind of place where good work can naturally happen. Of course, the administrator need not be the one who is refilling the staplers and purchasing reams of paper, but the administrator creates and facilitates an environment that functions, an environment that is fertile with new possibilities. Furthermore, the administrator does not attempt to micromanage every interaction and is not intimately wrapped up in every problem. He or she supports people in the environment to work through issues on their own as much as possible. Administration that takes its inspiration from the Divine Administrator knows how to remain in relationship with people while still leaving them free and responsible for their own actions.

Companion for the Journey: **Angela Merici**

Feast: **January 27**

The year was 1540 and Angela Merici knew that the time had come to give her final counsel to those entrusted with the care of the small community of women she had begun to gather around her five years earlier:

> This charge must not be a burden for you; on the contrary, you have to thank God most greatly that he has deigned to see to it that you are among those he wants to spend themselves in governing and safeguarding such a treasure [as] his own. . . . Do not be afraid of not knowing and not being able to do what is rightly required in such a singular government. Do something. Get moving. Be confident. Risk new things. Stick with it. Get on your knees. Then be ready for big surprises!

In her closing words, Angela reflects many of the characteristics we will discuss in this book: trust, courage, humility, hope, and—of course—breadth of vision. For Angela, these were characteristics that emerged not at once but over a long lifetime of diverse experiences.

Angela was born sometime around 1470 and lived the whole of her life in northern Italy on the eve of the Council of Trent. Although a contemporary of Michelangelo, Copernicus, and Christopher Columbus, Angela does not seem to have been concerned or affected so much by the artistic, scientific, or political intrigue of her day as by the struggles of poor Italian families, especially women, left in the wake of endless battles between various independent city-states. This was the hidden underside of Renaissance Europe, far from the spotlights of social intrigue.

Orphaned young, Angela never married, instead affiliating herself with the lay Franciscans, who were representative of a spiritual-renewal movement sweeping through Europe between the twelfth and sixteenth centuries. Large numbers of Christian lay people, wanting lives more closely modeled on the gospels, sought to pattern their days around prayer and care of the poor, espousing poverty and celibacy. Some of these laity affiliated themselves with new religious orders, such as the Franciscans or Dominicans. Some, such as the Beguines in northern Europe, were less structured.

For women in particular, the emergence of these new forms of discipleship was often liberating. Previously, European women had only two options available to them: marriage or the monastic cloister. Now they had the possibility of remaining single, engaged in the world, but dedicated to apostolic works. Many families, however, were nervous about what would happen to their daughters without the protection of a husband or a monastery. Church leaders were perplexed as to how to channel the diverse energies of the widespread movement in ways that wouldn't fragment the Church's unity or separate these lay people from official Church structures. As a result, lay initiatives were frequently viewed with suspicion and perceived as potentially dangerous.

Like many women of her time, Angela struggled to figure out the right place for herself in the Church and society. Because a significant part of her life was spent in pilgrimage, she witnessed firsthand various lay movements and gleaned new ideas from them. Yet, she had a difficult time finding a fit for her own situation in Brescia. At one point, she visited Rome, where a friend arranged for her a personal audience with the pope. Asked by the pope himself if she would settle in Rome and take leadership of an existing religious community, she considered the request but realized that this was not God's call for her and so returned north.

Angela's travel and reflection had led her to conceive of a new structure for women wanting to live the Christian life that would honor the impulse to be single and active in the world, while at the same time mitigating some of the fears of concerned family members and Church leaders. In Brescia, at the age of sixty-five, Angela finally organized a group of twenty-eight women to form the Company of St. Ursula—so named for a legendary saint from fourth-century England who gathered fellow women companions to make a pilgrimage that ended in martyrdom.

After making their joint commitment to one another, the women in the Company of St. Ursula did not live together in a convent but rather remained with their families or in small clusters on their own. They wore simple, ordinary clothes rather than a distinguishing habit. They individually supported themselves by their own labor, though when they died it was expected they would leave something to the company as a gift if they were able. Each committed to a life of personal prayer, which varied depending on whether the member could read or not.

Angela prepared a rule for the Company of St. Ursula to live by—the first religious rule known to have been written by a woman for women. In it she offered concrete guidelines about entrance into the company and about how the women were to relate to the wider society, as well as to their local parishes. She designed a structure for governance of the new company in which four members were elected to serve as spiritual guides—or *collonelles*—for the other women. They were to visit each member of the company every two weeks to see how she was doing and help her work through any challenges she faced. In addition, several older women and men from the town, not members of the company themselves, were elected to help members be able to advocate for themselves within a larger society not used to dealing with single women. These elders or matrons were to get involved if any of the members were being treated poorly by their families, needed legal assistance, or could not find a place to live. Angela was extremely practical about the needs single women would have when they became ill or were displaced from their homes when family members died, especially given that some company members were as young as twelve.

Angela spent the last five years of her life gathering and tending her fledgling new community, continuing to work on structures that would enable them to live as consecrated single women long after she was gone. In her final months, she dictated two sets of instructions. The first, called Angela's *Counsels*, was for the collonelles of the Company of St. Ursula. The second, called the *Legacies* or *Testament*, was for the matrons. In this document, Angela presciently notes,

> These being done, as well as other similar things, which the Holy Spirit will prompt, you to do according to times and circumstances, rejoice. . . . And if, according to the times and circumstances, the need arises to make new rules or do something differently, do it prudently and with good advice.

Angela models well the creativity and flexibility of God at the dawn of creation. She was able to see a future for herself and for other women that had not been tried before. With courage, she set about trying to build something with no architectural blueprints to rely upon. She sought to create an environment in which women of the Company of St. Ursula could flourish—with a light structure that enabled them to live with much freedom and independence, but also a safety net to catch them if they found themselves in trouble. In doing so, Angela provided not only a vision for the company, but also a practical day-to-day means of implementing that vision. Furthermore, she was open to allowing her work to evolve, not insisting that her own ideas be preserved for generations to come. The big picture of what God had planned for her company, she realized, might be larger than what even she could see.

For Reflection *and* Prayer

1. How has your experience of administration helped to expand your vision of the whole? In what specific ways has it stretched your heart to love more widely?

2. Can you think of or share the story of a time when you let go of your own agenda or aspiration because you realized, as administrator, that there was a larger common good?

3. Is there a situation in your administrative ministry at present where you may be challenged to take a broader view? What do you want to do about it?

4. What insights does the life of St. Angela offer in your efforts to live with a big-picture vision?

Divine Creator,
May the administrative work that I undertake
grow within me a greatness of vision,
enabling me to see the common good more
    clearly.
May it stir within me a greatness of spirit,
enabling me to love the common good more
    wholeheartedly.
In the weeks ahead, fashion my administrative
    ministry
to more closely reflect your intimate care for all of
    creation.
God of Eden's garden, show me what it means
to create an environment where all whom I serve
    can thrive.
Amen.

Administration calls us to . . .

2. Generativity

> Work thus belongs to the vocation of every person; indeed, a human being expresses and fulfills himself by working.
>
> —John Paul II
> *Centesimus Annus*, 6

Growing up, I was taught that work—much like the pain of childbearing and my intense fear of snakes—was a result of sin. Doesn't the Bible tell us so? It is right there in Genesis 3:14–19:

> Because you ate from the tree of which I had forbidden you to eat, Cursed be the ground because of you! In toil shall you eat its yield all the days of your life. . . . By the sweat of your face shall you get bread to eat, until you return to the ground, from which you were taken. (Gn 3:17–19)

It was only much later that I realized the expectation of work for humans actually precedes the Fall. Indeed, in Genesis 1, as soon as humans come into being, the very first words God speaks to them are, "Be fruitful and multiply, and fill the earth and subdue it; and have dominion over the fish of the sea and over the birds of the air and over every living thing that moves upon the earth" (Gn 1:28). This verse is difficult to translate and, as a result, is much debated. But, as many scholars today would note, the word "dominion" has its root in the Latin *domus* or "house." Humans, from the very start, are asked to tend the house of creation. This task comes to us, not as a curse, but as a privilege: we are honored among all creatures to be the Creator's image on planet Earth. We get to participate with God in the ongoing creation of the world. As a result of sin, our perspective toward this most basic human vocation may be distorted, and we may now experience work as drudgery or demeaning. But work has been part of God's plan for humanity from the very beginning—sin or no sin.

The Church's social teaching documents of the last hundred and twenty years have repeatedly emphasized that we must work in order to fulfill our most basic human vocation. We cannot reach our full human potential unless we are also fully engaged as "stewards of the house." In *Laborem Exercens,* John Paul II summarizes: "Work is a good thing for man—a good thing for his humanity—because through work man *not only transforms nature,* adapting it to his own needs, but he also *achieves fulfillment* as a human being and indeed, in a sense, becomes more a human being" (emphasis mine).

Italian educator Gianna Gobbi was keen to describe this more positive understanding of work using the image of a bee who, for the sake of its own flourishing, ceaselessly presses inward to the heart of the flower to suck its nectar and, in doing so, unwittingly covers its wings with the pollen that it will scatter across the fields in flight. The bee is nourished and grows by its labor, but so also the fruit tree and the vegetable patch.

The work of psychologist Erik Erikson in the past century very much confirms what the Church has intuited about the role human work can play both in the maturing of the person and in God's larger plan for creation. Erikson identified eight stages of development that all humans seem to pass through along the journey of a happy, wholesome life. These stages unfold as a series of crises in which life presents the person with an option to move toward greater maturity or not. These stages cannot be rushed (i.e., one cannot rush a six-year-old along to the same level of maturity expected of an eighty-year-old) nor can they be skipped (i.e., one cannot attain higher degrees of maturity without having confronted earlier crises). The seventh stage of development according to Erikson is acquired through confronting a crisis he defines as "generativity vs. stagnation." This lengthiest of the developmental phases is often associated with one's childbearing years and middle age. A person either enters into a "generative" phase where his or her life becomes oriented toward care for the ongoing flourishing of the world or turns in upon itself and worries only about his or her own personal needs. The phase of generativity certainly is not the first time a person contributes to the planet, but it is a phase in which the person does so intentionally and freely—without external pressure. Furthermore, it is a phase in which the person finds great joy in doing so. The generative person is often riddled with amazement: "How could this good come about through me? I played such a small role. There must be something greater at work here."

Many persons embrace generativity through the work of parenting offspring. Upon having children, they discover they no longer care so much about their own well-being as that of their daughters and sons. They find that their own greatest joy comes in seeing their children happy. But childbearing is not the only avenue for achieving generativity. Individuals also become generative through meaningful work. They give birth, not to a child, but to a novel, civic activism, a new park, improved access to health care for their city, an addition to the parish center, or the launch of a new curriculum. Through their work, they grow more and more into the person God dreams them to be while at the same time serving the next generation.

Administration offers endless opportunities to a person in the "generativity vs. stagnation" phase of life. It is a role in which one can generally get by simply by maintaining the status quo—not trying anything new or different. New ideas can easily be squashed on an administrator's desk before anyone else even finds out they were there. But at the same time, the administrator's desk is the place where new ideas can sprout, and the administrator is the one who gets to watch and water them in their infancy before anyone else even finds out they are there. This makes administration a very fertile field for someone with even the slightest amount of generative energy. Indeed, many find that the greater danger in administrative ministry is not stagnation but too many nascent projects crying for attention at the same time.

At what point does one become unsustainably generative? Erikson referred to choices against further development as "malignancies," but he also recognized that choosing too much progress could be dangerous. He termed these choices "maladaptions." I sometimes have to check, "Am I pacing myself as if I am running a sprint or a marathon?" If I catch myself sprinting all the time, I may need to stymie the generative impulse a bit.

But I must say that as much as they exhaust me and sometimes wear at my nerves, I love all my "children"—the biological child at home most dearly, but the figurative offspring on the administrative front are pretty great, too. In my line of work, the "office offspring"—my programs—evoke tenderness in my heart. I have loved nurturing them in their early days. I have loved seeing how different they are from what I first imagined they would be. I have loved watching them develop unique personalities and take off in directions I never foresaw. And at this phase, it is particularly delightful to observe a few of them prepare to go off on their own; they don't need my leadership anymore. I am a much better person for having parented them. In my old age, I will have many good stories to tell about them again and again, having forgotten the troubles they gave me but remembering the good. I am filled with wonder and amazement at what remarkable things have happened through these programs and projects far beyond my tiny efforts. How lucky to be a laborer in a field that belongs to the Lord, where some seeds never sprout, where some die before their time, but where some produce thirty, sixty, or even one hundred fold—more than we can ever imagine.

Companion for the Journey: **Jordan of Saxony**

Feast: **February 13**

If you have ever been brought aboard to replace a beloved leader, you know how hard it is to fill the shoes of the one who came before. Old loyalties are difficult to shift, new confidences tough to build. But if we find *our* transitions challenging, imagine what it would have been like to succeed St. Dominic, founder of the Order of Preachers.

Dominic de Guzman was one of the luminaries of his day. A Spanish priest born around the year 1170, Dominic became aware of how poor catechesis and preaching were leading to widespread misconceptions about the most basic tenets of the Catholic faith. This lack of formation in the faith resulted in divisions within the Church and even war. Dominic's response was to form a band of well-educated preachers who could persuasively address the theological questions of the day. This small band, initially gathered in southern France, spread quickly throughout the urban centers of Europe. Only months after receiving papal approval for the Order of Preachers in 1216, Dominic began sending waves of young brothers to Europe's newly founded universities on the conviction that, "hoarded up, the grain rots; cast to the winds it bears fruit."

Jordan first met Dominic's preachers when they arrived at the University of Paris in 1217. Jordan was probably about forty years old at the time and was a member of the teaching faculty at the university. Historians believe he may have originally been a mathematician before becoming a lecturer in the sacred sciences. In these early days of university life, all faculty and students were clerics, but this does not mean that all were priests or even intending to become priests. Many paused indefinitely along the way toward presbyteral ordination in one of the lower clerical ranks. Jordan, for instance, was a subdeacon.

Heavily engaged in the world of academia, it is unclear whether Jordan ever intended to pursue priesthood. But meeting the new Dominican arrivals on campus nudged him to consider the question further. Jordan was impressed by the preachers' zeal and commitment to their mission, as well as the high value they placed on study. On Ash Wednesday, in the year 1220, Jordan and a friend, Henry of Marbourg, marched into the priory during Mass and asked to receive the Dominican habit.

The Dominicans identified Jordan's giftedness for administration and leadership very quickly. Only two months after entering the Order of Preachers, he was elected to serve as a representative to the general chapter in Bologna. The following year, he was again chosen. At that second meeting, the Dominicans decided to structure their new order into eight provinces across Europe, and Jordan was chosen to serve as provincial for the region of Lombardy—the largest of the provinces, with the city of Bologna as its hub. Bologna was the site of one of Europe's most prestigious universities, and furthermore it was the city that Dominic had come to use as his home base. Jordan later wrote: "This office was imposed on me when, having spent only one year in the order, I had hardly begun to take root in it. Before I had learned how to deal with my own imperfections, here was I sent to govern others."

After his election, Jordan returned to Paris to pack and say goodbye before returning to Bologna. Imagine his shock and dismay to discover that during his journey Dominic had died of a fever. Jordan's year as provincial in Lombardy was dedicated to following up on plans Dominic had intended for the region. He founded four more Dominican houses and continued conversations Dominic had begun about a monastery for women in Bologna. When the time for the annual general chapter rolled around again in the spring, Jordan was elected master general, the successor to Dominic. It was May 22, 1222. Jordan had been in the Order of Preachers just over two years, and he was now responsible for all eight of the order's provinces, a total of forty priories.

During the next fifteen years, Jordan continued to nurture the seeds Dominic had planted and to bring them to a point where they were sturdy enough to flourish on their own. Several key qualities mark his administration. The first is itinerancy. While Jordan continued the use of Bologna as a home base, he was rarely there since he traveled unceasingly, opening new Dominican priories and enlarging existing ones. Jordan regularly traversed what now constitutes France, Germany, Brussels, and Italy. He promoted missions in Poland, Greece, Romania, and the Middle East. Early in his travel, he contracted a serious fever—perhaps malaria—that continued to resurface periodically throughout the rest of his life. Yet, Jordan continued to travel, and the best estimates suggest that 240 Dominican priories were founded under his leadership.

A second characteristic of Jordan's administration was a sense of levelheadedness. Jordan was not one to get caught up in the frenzy of success or the pitfalls of disillusionment during the heady early days of the movement. "Happy is the man who keeps to the golden mean," he once wrote, "giving everything its proper measure." He discouraged the brothers from getting wrapped up in the miraculous, the flashy, and the polemical.

Jordan's administration was also characterized by commitment to the intellectual formation of his men. Jordan was enthused about the rapid growth in the order, but numbers were not enough. The preachers also had to be well educated. He was able to attain two chairs for Dominican faculty at the University of Paris and one at Oxford. Yet, recognizing that not all his brothers would be able to study with university faculty, he worked to establish the placement of a theologian in each priory to teach and serve as a resource.

A final characteristic of Jordan's administration was the value he placed on friendship. Jordan did not allow his leadership to isolate him from others. He relied on friends for support, comfort, and advice in his ministry. He maintained his lifelong friendship with Henry of Marbourg, who went on to serve as prior of Cologne. Indeed, according to some accounts Henry died in Jordan's arms after a sudden illness.

Perhaps the friendship for which Jordan is most remembered is his friendship with Diana d'Andalo, the young woman with whom Dominic had initially discussed the possibility of a monastery for women in Bologna. Diana wanted women to be able to serve as prayer and study partners in the preaching mission. She made vows in Dominic's presence, but it took several more years for her to acquire the property and resources needed to launch St. Agnes Monastery. Jordan became a faithful supporter of Diana and her sisters, even when some of the other Dominican men hesitated to endorse the effort. In return, Diana became a great support to Jordan. Their extensive correspondence over the course of thirteen years testifies to the way that they cared for and relied upon each other throughout the trials each faced in administration.

Indeed, the last letter Jordan ever wrote was a letter to Diana from somewhere in the Middle East. Following the 1236 general chapter, Jordan decided he should visit the Dominican priories emerging in Palestine. It is unclear how long he was gone or where he went. He likely stopped in Cyprus, Jerusalem, and possibly Tripoli. In this last letter, Jordan wrote, "O Diana, how miserable is the present state which we must endure since we cannot love one another without sorrow or think of one another without anxiety! Who shall lead us . . . into the City of the Lord of Hosts, where we shall sigh no more, sighing neither after the Most High, nor for one another?"

It seems unlikely the letter ever reached Diana. She died of illness sometime in late 1236. Jordan meanwhile departed from what is now northern Israel, in a ship bound for Naples. He was scheduled to preach to the university students in Padua during Lent. But his ship encountered stormy weather, and ninety-nine passengers aboard, including Jordan, drowned. The date was February 13, 1237.

Jordan had managed not only to ably fill the shoes of Dominic, but he even died still active on behalf of Dominic's cause. In doing so, he models well the quality of generativity. His was a life that was lived for a mission in which he wholeheartedly believed—a mission that gave him great passion and energy, even as he spent himself in its service. Tragic though his death may seem, he likely would not have had it any other way. He was able to do what gave him joy until the very end.

For Reflection *and* Prayer

1. What is your attitude toward work? Does your work evoke images of curse or blessing for you? In what ways does your administrative ministry give you the opportunity to experience work as generative?

2. Can you recall and tell the story of a time in your work as an administrator when you faced a moment of decision between generativity and stagnation, and you chose generativity? How did this feel?

3. Which is a greater danger for you, the malignancy of stagnation or the maladaption of over-generativity?

What most hinders you from being able to exercise generativity in a consistently healthy and wholesome way?

4. What insights does the life of Blessed Jordan of Saxony offer regarding joyful generativity?

O Holy Trinity,
All of creation exists as an overflow of your divine energy.
Made in your image, I share in your creativity.
I know what it means to be so full of passion and energy
that sparks begin to fly and new things emerge that were not there before.
I ask you to nourish and sustain the energy within me, O Triune God,
that I continue to freely and joyfully serve the mission of my institution.
May those around me experience my office as life-giving and fruitful,
rather than life-draining and sterile.
In the gift of myself to others, may I discover my own deepest purpose.
Amen.

Administration calls us to . . .

3. Trust

> We do not know what we should do, but our eyes are fixed upon thee.
>
> —2 Chronicles 20:12

As I travel the country asking administrators what they have learned in their work, the most common response, often after a long pause, is "trust." The frequency of the response eventually has led me to laugh. Possibly, as a group, those of us with a proclivity for administration are not naturally very trusting people! Perhaps the laughter here should be primarily directed toward myself as the draw toward administration in my case involves a love of order and desire to see things done right. I like to see processes flow smoothly. I like when things run like clockwork. And, deep down inside, I harbor the conviction that the best chance for that happening is if I am intimately involved, controlling all the details.

After thirteen years, my job has almost beaten that out of me—not quite, but almost. Many days in my office resemble a three-ring circus on methamphetamines. "I try to take it one day at a time," a popular bumper sticker quips, "but sometimes several days attack me at once." Administration has placed me in situations larger than what I am able to handle on my own. In doing so, administration has forced me to let go of the illusion that I can successfully manage every detail and taught me to trust others to carry out their part.

At the beginning of an administrative relationship, it can sometimes be hard to entrust others with important jobs to do on their own, in the way they see fit. Wouldn't it be good for her to observe a little longer? What if he does something that offends the congregation or the client? What if she fails and I have to pick up the pieces? It can be hard to turn over portions of our ministry—especially those portions in which we feel particularly competent—and allow others to do them differently. It's hard to allow the possibility that things might go awry—to let go of control over how the work will be done. But, eventually, we realize that God has been gracious in abundantly distributing gifts throughout the human race, not merely among administrators. Others cannot gain needed experience in their positions if we insist on doing all the work for them. And, furthermore, they likely have gifts that we do not. The work will be more successful and enduring because of others' contributions, not less.

As a complement to learning to trust others, administration also teaches us to trust ourselves. This is a good bit different than doing things ourselves or believing we know the one right way to do something. A number of administrators I have talked to frame it more or less like this: "It used to take me lots and lots of time to make sure I had all my ducks in a row. I needed to make sure every last detail was in place and leave nothing to chance. I made sure I had the answer to every question, whether or not the question had been asked. Now I am more comfortable winging it. I am more comfortable knowing that I can be flexible in the moment, that I can trust my gut response. And even if I don't know all the answers, I am at ease saying, 'Let me get back to you' and realizing people are okay with that."

Many administrators admit that the greatest act of trust that has been required of them is learning to trust the value of the ministry itself. While we might go into administration hoping to make a difference, to set an institution on a new course, to offer clear direction, we find that much of administration is about sustaining, keeping what already exists going—in common jargon: "paper pushing." Many days, I have sworn that as soon as I clear off my desk, I will think a great new thought. But as soon as I clear things off the desk, more material keeps coming in. I delete three e-mails, and during the time that it takes me to do so, four more arrive. Day after day goes by when I marvel that I continue to get paid, because I have no evidence that anything has been accomplished at all. I keep trying to bring order out of chaos, but chaos keeps bobbing up again, as in the carnival game Whack-a-Mole. I wonder, does anything I do really make a difference?

There is a certain poverty in administrative ministry. It is not a poverty of money (though definitely many ministry positions push the boundaries here). Rather, it is a poverty of measurable results, a poverty of visible outcomes. A pastor with whom I interned once told me, "I can see now why so many pastors like building things—gyms, church buildings, new science wings on the school, even wheelchair ramps. So much of our work never produces any visible results. It feels good to be able to watch something physically tangible take shape once in a while!"

Ultimately, this kind of day-to-day experience in administration results in a trust of God. We learn to trust that God is always quietly at work, moving within the system in ways that we can't see. Even when it feels as if nothing we do is making a difference, God is working behind the scenes. And when we least expect it, something brilliant happens. A grant comes through, or a seemingly insurmountable obstacle dissipates. A long-awaited contract materializes. A juggernaut is resolved. And you know that it had nothing to do with you. God has been taking care of things all along.

I remember that when I first began my job at the school, it used to cause me a great deal of anxiety. I would walk into my office and be overwhelmed by a sense of panic. Where to start? What to do first? I remember observing our school's president at the time, how almost every day he would come out and eat lunch with students, staff, and faculty in the lounge, never seeming rushed or nervous, even though I knew he had every reason to be. I wondered how he managed to sleep at night, given all he had to deal with, but like Jesus, he seemed to have developed the capacity to sleep through storms. It wasn't that he was detached or didn't care about what happened—and there were days when he was angry and anxious. But most days, he exuded a sense of calm. "I've been around the block enough times to know it is going to be okay," he would say. His years in administration had mellowed him. He'd learned most storms aren't quite as fierce as they appear. If you talk to them, they will respond in kind. He had learned to trust the people who worked for him, his own capacity to work through most anything, and the basic goodness of God's world.

Companion for the Journey: **Louise de Marillac**

Feast: **March 15**

Histories of seventeenth-century France reveal a vibrant yet conflicted society. As the Thirty Years' War devastated neighboring territories, the French faced their own internal struggles between the monarchy and aristocrats, the landowners and the landless, the urban city dwellers and the countryside peasants. Poverty was widespread. A renewed religiosity spurred on by the Council of Trent led to an increased desire to assist the poor, but efforts to help were unorganized and the approach unsystematic.

The charitable impulses of the age are well captured in the image of a peasant priest named Vincent de Paul. A large-hearted man, Vincent witnessed the plight of many poor families, especially around the Paris region. One of Vincent's key insights was that "the poor suffer less from lack of generosity than from lack of organization." Toward that end, he had begun a variety of projects among priests and among the elites to see what could be done. But he needed a partner—a collaborator with strong organization and networking skills. He needed Louise de Marillac.

Louise de Marillac's complicated childhood reflects much of the tension and promise of her time. Louise was born in 1591, the illegitimate child of an aristocratic father and an unknown mother. The father acknowledged Louise as his offspring and provided for her financially, but he was uninvolved in her upbringing. Louise was raised in a monastery and then, upon the death of her father, was placed under the guardianship of a politically active uncle, who transferred her to a boarding home. Louise was regarded as a quiet, reflective child, perhaps with a propensity for depression.

As a teen, Louise was attracted to the monastic life and vowed to become a nun, but the order of her choice refused her for reasons history does not record. Instead, Louise's guardian arranged a marriage with Antoine de Gras—the private secretary of the Queen Mother. The marriage, like many aristocratic marriages of the time, was intended to serve both families' political purposes rather than the desires of the heart, yet the match was a happy one. Louise gave birth to a son, Michel, less than a year after the wedding. Born prematurely, Michel seems to have had special needs. He definitely had a difficult and erratic personality that caused Louise much anxiety throughout her life.

Nine years into their marriage, Antoine became seriously ill. The stress of his illness and the challenges of raising Michel alone wore mightily on Louise. She appears to have slipped into a period of serious depression, made more acute by her fear that her familial sufferings were a punishment from God for breaking her teenage vow to become a nun. On the feast of Pentecost in 1623, Louise had a powerful prayer experience that led her finally to begin to trust that she was where she was supposed to be and that God had plans for her. The experience was so memorable and brought her such peace that Louise wrote about it on a piece of paper that she kept folded in her pocket for many years, and she is said to have read it whenever she felt that trust wavering.

Shortly thereafter, Louise was paired with Vincent de Paul as her spiritual director and discovered that she shared with him a common concern for the poor. Following the death of her husband in 1625, Louise became involved in Vincent's efforts to create Confraternities of Charity—bands of aristocratic women who would assist with projects to meet the needs of the poor. Vincent had begun founding such groups as a way to continue the positive energy created by his preaching. Some of the confraternities became dynamic and self-sustaining, but others faced serious challenges when he moved on to preach elsewhere.

Vincent decided to send Louise as his ambassador to various confraternities to help rejuvenate their energy and to work through organizational problems.

Repeatedly, Louise observed that when confraternity women went into the homes of those they served, they had a difficult time relating across the classes. Unused to the cramped space and odors, they feared for their health and began sending their servants instead of visiting themselves. The servants generally were efficient and effective in their interactions, but they showed little compassion. Louise suspected that the gulf between the classes might be too great for the confraternities to bridge. She and Vincent needed to somehow partner the financial resources and connections of the confraternities with the practical know-how and gumption of women not accustomed to wealth, and they needed to make sure that all interactions with the poor were permeated with compassion. In her mind, Louise began to envision a religious community of peasant women who could comfortably enter into the homes of the poor and serve their needs.

The first woman to collaborate with Louise in this regard was Marguerite Naseau, a peasant woman Vincent met during one of his preaching missions. Louise was enthused by the emerging possibilities, but Vincent was unconvinced. Religious life had traditionally been a call for women from wealthy families, who could provide dowries that would give the religious community financial stability. The sudden death of Marguerite from an illness contracted in her ministry added to Vincent's hesitancy. But during his annual retreat, Vincent was moved to reconsider.

By November 1633, Louise gathered a small group of five peasant women within her own home to begin living a communal life with them. They called themselves the Daughters of the Charities—referring to their relationship with the Confraternities of Charity—or sometimes just the Daughters. Louise did not envision them as an official religious order with cloistered living quarters and a rigorous prayer schedule. Rather, they were women who shared elements of a common life and a common mission with each other but who remained in the world. There was no term for this kind of life in the French Church's vocabulary. It took a great act of trust on Louise's part to believe such a thing could be accepted. Eventually, Louise and the others decided to take vows of poverty, celibacy, obedience, and service to the poor—but these vows were not the formal, permanent vows of a religious order. Instead, they were personal vows—the kind that any Christian might privately make—taken for just one year at a time.

With growth, however, Louise faced a number of administrative challenges. The community rapidly grew to the point that Louise had to persuade Vincent to purchase a new home for them across the street from his own. Sometimes it was difficult to discern the motivations of the women who asked to join the community. Did they truly desire to serve the poor, or did they simply want to move to the city, away from dire home situations? The women's lack of education and spiritual formation could make community life difficult. Sometimes the confraternity members tried to make the women into their personal servants, asking them to attend to personal needs rather than the needs of the poor. Parish priests, as well, wanted the women under their own command, rather than affiliated with Louise.

The years 1646 and 1647 were a time of particular crisis for the young community. The original zeal of the founding years seems to have waned, and over the course of a mere eighteen months, one-sixth of the members left. Louise's secretary wrote of this period: "It seemed like God wanted to empty the house." Louise's angst was heightened by challenges with her young adult son, who at varying points in time had run away, threatened to commit suicide, and taken up with the daughter of a wine merchant.

Still, Louise was undeterred. She worked to create a strong formation program for new members. As the Daughters began to go out and live in the various parishes of Paris in small groups, she made frequent visits. As they moved out beyond Paris, she wrote frequent letters. While she remained in close friendship with Vincent, she slowly became less reliant on him and more trusting of her own capacities, as well as more trusting of God's.

Letters and stories from the closing decade of Louise's life reveal how the many years of organization, leadership, and struggle had mellowed Louise's temperament. Whereas her early writing is marked by a sense of urgency and energy—but also angst and extreme sensitivity—Louise's later writing reflects an assertive yet calm tenacity. "Do not be upset if things are not as you would want them to be for a long time to come," she said. "Do the little you can very peacefully and calmly so as to allow room for the guidance of God in your lives. Do not worry about the rest."

In her final years, Louise was blessed to witness the expansion of her community beyond the French borders and to receive the official approval of the Daughters of Charity as a new sort of religious congregation. She was also blessed with the joy of seeing Michel finally marry and the birth of a granddaughter—Louise Renee—in 1651. Louise died peacefully on March 15, 1660—six months before Vincent. Their lifelong collaboration had changed the face of compassion in seventeenth-century France and far beyond.

For Reflection *and* Prayer

1. Has your experience of administration increased your sense of trust in others? In yourself? In your ministry? In God?

2. Can you recall a time when your work as an administrator invited you to trust, and things worked out better than you had expected?

3. Is there a situation in your current administrative ministry in which you may be challenged to increase your readiness to trust? How will you address this?

4. What insights do you take from the life of St. Louise regarding the invitation to trust?

Gracious God,
Creation overflows with your goodness.
Where I see only scarcity, you tell me to look closer,
hinting at a hidden abundance.
Teach me to look at the world through your eyes.
Help me to be aware of all the ways you care for my institution

beyond my view, beyond my comprehension.
Make evident the giftedness with which you have showered your people.
Help me to recognize in myself and in those with whom I serve
the multiplicity of talents and possibilities if I but trust.
Amen.

Administration calls us to . . .

4. Agape

And we ourselves shall be loved for a while and forgotten. But the love will have been enough; all those impulses of love return to the love that made them. Even memory is not necessary for love. There is the land of the living and a land of the dead, and the bridge is love, the only survival, the only meaning.

—Thornton Wilder
The Bridge of San Luis Rey

At the close of Thornton Wilder's 1927 classic *The Bridge of San Luis Rey*, the abbess sits alone with her thoughts. She has lost a young mentee in whom she placed much hope, and she perceives that all of her progressive efforts on behalf of women and youth, the disabled and mentally ill, will not make any lasting difference if she has no successor. The abbess realizes that she is one of the only persons left to remember the deceased girl, and that when she herself dies, no one will remember her either. Is loving worth the effort when it seems so fruitless?

Although we probably do not often say it aloud, we likely share similar meanderings at times. Don't we assume that loving others will bring us joy? That it will be gratifying and meaningful? That good things will come of it? That it portends a future filled with hope? Is it really love if it doesn't leave us feeling fulfilled?

Unfortunately, the English language does not possess the nuance around the term "love" that many other languages do. Greek—the language of the New Testament—offers at least four different words to describe what, in English, would all fall under the umbrella of that one word. Greek distinguishes between the passion felt by lovers, the fondness shared among friends or siblings, and the protection of parents for their offspring. In addition, it has a word for that mysterious choice humans can make to care about the well-being of others with whom they share no familial or friendship bonds.

The first three types of love engage the emotions—indeed, they rely on the presence of feelings. No true friendship can exist between two persons who don't enjoy being with one another. Romance, by definition, is not romance if there is no attraction involved. But the last type of love—*agape*—has very little to do with feeling at all. It is an act of the will. Agape could be described as a "disinterested love," not because one isn't interested in the other, but because one's own self-interests are not necessarily met in the relationship. Agape is a commitment to the best interest of the other, even if one receives little or nothing in return.

In the Christian scriptures, it is the last of these terms—agape—that is most frequently used to describe the nature of Christian love. Disciples of Jesus are not expected to like everyone or feel deeply satisfied by their interactions with others. Loving might not leave them feeling peaceful or happy. Christian love is not a feeling; it is a consistent choice. And this love has a value all its own, as the abbess in Wilder's novel finally concludes—not because it makes us feel better or results in anything good, but because the act of loving is itself good. This love lingers long after the persons involved are gone. In the end, we might say that love is eternal because God—the Eternal One—permeates this kind of love. 1 John 4 tells us, "God is agape" and "those who live in agape live in God and God in them."

Life is filled with opportunities to practice this kind of love, and hence to know God. A life in administration, however, offers perhaps an extraordinary number of opportunities. The nature of administration involves a great deal of behind-the-scenes work. Whereas the teacher is able to get to know her students and develop affection for them, and the social worker regularly interacts face-to-face with his clients, administrators often don't have a great deal of interaction with those whom their institutions serve. The principal sometimes doesn't get to know the names of all the children, much less their stories. The CEO of a hospital may never even see the names of patients—much less connect them with faces. Granted, it is sometimes easier to love humanity from a distance! But often one of the greatest poverties of administration can be knowing people only through a computer screen. I think frequently of the remarkable superintendent of Catholic high schools that I knew in my diocese—a generous and kind priest pouring out his lifeblood day after day for lots of teens who didn't even know he existed.

More than many professions, administration offers the opportunity to grow in the capacity for agape. By its very character, administration encourages the practice of giving oneself freely and abundantly without always knowing what good one has done or who has been touched. It urges one to love without expecting any emotional gratification in return. Many days, as I organize the projects of the day before me on my desk, I find myself leaning toward those that would put me in contact with people I like, persons whom it is desirable to serve. And if I do something for them, I can be pretty sure they'll pay me back in turn. But then I find myself asking, "Self, which of these tasks most deserves your energy today, not because anyone will notice and say 'thank you' but because it is a good to be done? What will you do purely out of love for someone who will never even know?" Practicing tiny acts of agape day after day, even in something so simple as how we prioritize our tasks, slowly gives us deeper insight into the words of the Christian Gospel about agape, and it nudges us in the direction of ever-greater generosity.

In the twelfth century, the Jewish philosopher Maimonides outlined his insights into the development of generosity in a person. He said that the lowest level of generosity was giving to another unwillingly. The second level was giving to another willingly, but less than what one could give. The third level of generosity was giving only after being asked. The fourth level was giving without being asked. The fifth level of generosity was giving to a recipient one does not know, but who knows the giver. The sixth level was giving to a recipient that the giver knows, but who does not know the giver. Maimonides regarded the highest levels of giving as giving in situations when neither party knows the other, and when it moves the receiver toward self-reliance so that she or he no longer needs to rely on the charity of another. In many ways, administration allows persons to practice giving at some of the highest levels of generosity. It offers us opportunities to practice agape in profound ways.

Companion for the Journey: **Richard of Chichester**

Feast: **April 3**

"Richard of Chichester" will be a rather obscure name for most administrators, but anyone who has ever seen a production of *Godspell* will quickly recognize the famous prayer attributed to him on his deathbed in 1253:

> Thanks be to thee, my Lord Jesus Christ, for all the benefits thou hast given me, for all the pains and insults thou has born for me. O most merciful Redeemer, friend and brother, may I know thee more clearly, love thee more dearly, follow thee more nearly.

This closing plea of Richard's captures well the single-hearted devotion with which he lived his life.

He was born Richard de la Wyche near Droitwich, England, in 1197. His family surname derived from the salt springs clustered around the family estate.

Richard's propensity for administration appeared early in life. After the premature death of his parents while he and his siblings were quite young, guardians mismanaged the family property, bringing it into disrepair. Richard's older brother, the intended inheritor of the estate, was unable to turn the situation around, so Richard stopped his own education to manage the farm. Within a few years, the estate was so prosperous that his brother offered to turn the inheritance over to Richard. But having given the estate a sound economic footing, Richard instead chose to return to his studies, now at Oxford.

Others quickly recognized Richard's administrative gifts as well. After further studies at Paris and Bologna, Richard was asked to serve as the chancellor of the University of Oxford in 1235. When his university classmate Edmund Rich became Archbishop of Canterbury, he asked Richard to come serve as the chancellor of the archdiocese. Edmund was an outspoken bishop often at odds with other key political and ecclesial figures of the time. King Henry III proved a particularly challenging nemesis for Edmund, refusing to fill empty episcopal positions throughout England so as to make the Church collections that usually would have gone to support a bishop his own. Richard was one of Edmund's closest advisors through all of these struggles and provided him legal counsel. When Edmund announced a journey to Rome for an upcoming council, Richard was one of the few who traveled with him, and when Edmund became ill en route, Richard nursed him through his final days.

Thinking he might retire from administration following his friend's death, Richard went to live with the Dominican community in Orléans and continued his studies in theology. He was ordained a priest in 1243 and tried his hand at parish ministry in a small church in Kent. Almost immediately, however, the new archbishop of Canterbury, Boniface, asked Richard to resume the role of archdiocesan chancellor. The remainder of Richard's life was spent in ecclesial administration, confronting degrees of political and economic complication that would frustrate even the most seasoned administrator.

In 1244, the bishop of Chichester—a small town on the southern coast of England near modern-day Portsmouth—died. The canons of the Chichester cathedral elected Robert Passelewe to fill the role, but Boniface and others petitioned the pope to annul this election in favor of Richard, on account of Robert's want of learning. Richard traveled to Rome to receive the pope's blessing, but upon returning to England he discovered that Henry III had locked him out of the bishop's residence and absconded with the diocesan revenues. For almost two years, Richard was homeless within his own diocese, relying on the hospitality of local priests. He became known for his simple lifestyle and diet, traveling through the diocese barefoot, preaching on street corners and open fields. After two years, Henry finally recognized Richard as bishop, under threat of papal excommunication, but Richard's ascetic lifestyle remained much the same.

Richard's administrative talents helped bring the diocese to a new level of organization and service. He held his priests to high levels of accountability, cracking down on abuses against celibacy and unprofessional appearance. He demanded the sacraments be administered generously, without payment. In return, he also sought to protect the rights of priests against abuse; knights were given severe penances for attacking a priest. He worked to increase reverence for and regular participation in the liturgy. Richard also insisted on basic catechesis for all the laity. He instituted a harvest tithe in all parishes to support the efforts of the diocese, much of which was then given in alms to the poor. Because of his efficient stewardship of finances, he was named a collector of the subsidy for the pope's crusades in 1250. He was also asked to oversee the building of a church in memory of his friend Edmund Rich in Dover.

But amid all of his many administrative efforts, Richard does not appear to have lost his ability to relate to people at a very personal level. He was known for his cheerfulness and enjoyment of the simple things of life, such as the songs of birds. Although the work of his office was great, he was known to balance it with the activity of gardening. The orchard next to the bishop's residence, still viewable today, is rumored to have been planted by him. Legend has it that Richard harbored a particular fascination with growing figs.

Richard died in Dover in 1253. He had traveled to the southeast corner of the country in order to consecrate the church of St. Edmund, but he caught fever en route. He persisted in consecrating the building on April 2 but then died on April 3. He was canonized less than a decade later.

Richard is one of the few saints on the Church's calendar to be honored solely for the holiness he practiced in ministry of administration. He was not martyred. He was not known to work miracles during his lifetime. He did not write any famous books or leave any remarkable sermon texts. He did not found a new religious congregation. He was simply the bishop of a small diocese in the south of England during a chaotic time in the history of that diocese. He helped to bring some sense of order into the situation. Richard's life reflects an agape love that was exercised primarily through administrative tasks such as oversight of buildings, creation of personnel policies, and institution of liturgical norms—tasks far from the spotlight, the kinds of tasks with which we administrators are all too familiar.

For Reflection *and* Prayer

1. What has your experience of administration taught you about the mystery of love and its many faces?
2. Can you tell the story of a time when you poured out your energy for another or others who never even knew how much of yourself you were giving to them? How did this feel? Why did you do it?
3. Is there a situation in your administrative ministry at present where you think God may be inviting you to love more freely, without reward, without recognition? What will you do about this?
4. Does the life of St. Richard offer you any clues as to what it might mean to live agape as a way of life?

Eternal God,

In a world that is constantly changing, your love alone remains steadfast.

No matter the shift, no matter the twist, no matter the loss, no matter even the harshness

of death, your love lingers—free, abundant, forever.
May my administrative work participate in your divine love for all humankind.
May it offer me the possibility to do good for others without counting the cost.
And may it nudge me toward true generosity of spirit.
Holy Bridge that unites us one to another,
may the ministry of administration cultivate within me genuine Christian love.
Amen.

Administration calls us to . . .

5. Integrity

The only appropriate response to privilege is absolute integrity.

—John O'Donohue
"The Inner Landscape of Beauty"
On Being with Krista Tippett

About fifteen years ago now, I remember digging through my refrigerator and opening a Tupperware container of cream cheese that had clearly taken up residence in the back corner of the bottom shelf for far too long. Greeted by a mound of green, fuzzy mold with an odor that could clear the neighbor's sinuses, I exclaimed something fit only for a sailor's ears. You may wonder why this event stands out in my mind when it took place so long ago. Surely I have had many a sour container in my fridge since then, and surely there have been other times when my language has been less than edifying. The reason why I remember this particular afternoon is because my toddler son was there. He was two years old—in that very phase of life known for rapid acquisition of language. And for weeks thereafter, he would go into the refrigerator opening containers and repeating my scandalous choice of words. The language hadn't bothered me before, but when I saw him try it on for size, it felt terribly inappropriate. I realized I would have to clean up my act, if not for myself, then for him.

Many parents can tell similar stories. I know my uncle stopped smoking when his child asked him about cigarettes. My husband is much more observant of the speed limit now that our son is studying for his driver's license. Administrators tell parallel tales. There is nothing like being responsible for the execution of policies to make one start following them. When we are charged with challenging others to live healthy, wholesome lives at the service of the common good, we will be immediately confronted with all those ways that we are not as healthy, wholesome, or cooperative as we should be.

For example, how can I talk with a student about developing better balance in her life when I work seventy hours a week? How can I suggest an employee talk to a counselor about possible depression when I've assiduously avoided counselors myself? How can I give lectures on good conflict management when I absolutely refuse to deal constructively with a coworker? How do I demand paperwork be turned in by the deadline when I habitually procrastinate and ask for extensions? As we hold up the mirror for others, they—often unwittingly—hold the mirror up to us. We see where greater personal integrity is needed between what we advocate and what we actually do.

Integrity is a quality easy to spot in others but often not easy to acquire for oneself. Even young children are quick to spot lapses of integrity in their parents. Students are quick to identify hypocrisy in their teachers, employees in their bosses. But rarely can one see hypocrisy in oneself unless one is open to allowing others to help illuminate it. Through annual reviews, patient feedback, student evaluations, and endless other means, administration offers plentiful opportunities to have our incongruences made visible to us. It can make us attentive to aspects of our own life that we might otherwise overlook or relegate to the unimportant category.

Of course, whether administration actually helps us to grow in integrity or not depends on how we respond to having these incongruences illuminated. One well-trafficked road, always available to us, is defensiveness. But a less congested route is also always open—the route of honesty and willingness to change behaviors. Seeing the incongruence with our own eyes and witnessing the impact in the lives of others is different than just having been told about it. The desire for change becomes more than just an intellectual assent, "Yes, yes, I'll have to work on that." It registers in the gut: "Wow, I'm really going to have to do something different!" Sometimes, as the preacher Fred Craddock says, "the longest trip a person takes is that from head to heart." But once that trip has been made, the hardest part of the journey is already over and the impetus to continue is strong.

Administrators who accept the challenge of integrity in their work become remarkable—albeit sometimes unwelcome—gifts to the institutions that they serve. Their ability to see and tell the truth about themselves puts them in a unique position of also being able to see and tell the truth about the institution and incongruences that may exist between what the institution professes and what it actually does.

Scripture scholar Walter Wink notes that in the biblical worldview, every institution, like every individual person, exists to serve some divine purpose. Every institution has a God-given vocation. In New Testament times, this realization was often couched in language of the angelic and demonic. Just as persons might be thought to have guardian angels who watch out for their divine vocation, so do institutions. For example, the book of Revelation includes seven letters written to various Christian churches. The letters are not addressed to the membership of each church—which will wax and wane, shift and change, over time—but the church's "angel." An angel, in Wink's understanding, is the spirit of the institution, which remains somewhat stable even as individual persons within the institution change. Angels are the bearers of the community's God-given purpose. But as Wink points out, angels can fall. The spirit of an institution can become unfaithful to its original vocation and turn demonic. Institutions, like persons, can lose their integrity.

Because they are behind the scene and because they behold the big picture administrators are generally in very close contact with their institution's invisible angel. They are able to see things to which the public eye is not privy. They are able to tell whether the spiritual core of the institution is in harmony with the mission-and-values statement that hangs on the wall. Administrators who have committed themselves to personal integrity can play a significant role in helping their institutions commit to institutional integrity, for these are the people who have taken the journey themselves and know what it looks like.

The author James Baldwin once said that to become a great novelist one must be willing "to tell as much of the truth as one can bear, and then a little more." Surely the same could be said of holy administrators. Our work beckons us to practice a degree of honesty most would find fearsome, and yet it beckons us all the same.

Companion for the Journey: **Bruno**

Feast: **October 6**

St. Bruno may seem a strange choice for a book on administration. If you recognize his name at all, you probably know him as the founder of the Carthusians—a small community of hermits, now almost a thousand years old. Bruno's vocation story, however, is a complex one that spans multiple forms of service in the Church. Indeed, Bruno provides an excellent model of living integrity in the midst of various requests and demands made on him by Church leaders—some of which were legitimate and some less so.

Bruno was born in the city of Cologne, in modern-day Germany, around the year 1030, but he was educated in Reims, one of the great intellectual centers at the time. Upon finishing his studies, Bruno became a secular canon—a priest who ministered within the diocesan Church while sharing a common life with other priests. Canons received their own income and owned their own homes, but they would pray the Liturgy of the Hours with each other daily in the cathedral.

In 1056, while Bruno was still in his twenties, the archbishop appointed him director of studies, a role not unlike the modern superintendent of schools. Bruno held this position for two decades. He became renowned as a lecturer and was well loved by his students at the cathedral school, several of whom would become prominent figures in the emerging age of Gregorian Reform.

This reform, named for its chief advocate, Pope Gregory VII, intended to address the political quagmire in which the eleventh-century Church found itself muddled. Church offices, originally filled by popular election of the faithful, had come to be appointed by local political leaders—no longer on the basis of holiness and recognized gifts for leadership, but rather for political gain. All too often, episcopal positions—which obviously involved a great deal of power and stewardship of large amounts of wealth—were simply purchased by the highest bidder, a practice known as simony. Efforts to change the way bishops were appointed met great resistance among those who had purchased their offices, as well as political leaders heavily invested in maintaining the status quo.

Bruno and his students inevitably found themselves entangled in these controversies. In 1067, the archbishop of Reims died, opening the door for Manassès of Gournay to assume the episcopacy. That Manassès attained the position through simony is undisputed, but in his early years Manassès worked hard to nurture good relations with Rome, and Gregory entrusted him with a number of delicate diplomatic tasks. Publicly, Manassès appeared charitable and magnanimous, but those who worked with him on a daily basis knew otherwise. They experienced Manassès as haughty and deceptive, violent in his language and dirty in his politicking. When complaints were filed against him with the pope, he made gestures of reconciliation with his diocesan staff. One of these was appointing Bruno—a person of stellar reputation—as his chancellor in 1075. But Bruno quickly caught on to the duplicity in Manassès's administrative style.

In 1076, Bruno and several other diocesan staff members filed an official complaint with Rome against the archbishop, putting their positions and livelihood at risk. They were compelled to go into hiding in the home of a local count while the charges against Manassès were slowly processed. In 1077, the pope's legate convened a council. Bruno testified, but Manassès refused to show up. The legate suspended Manassès from his position, but Manassès appealed directly to the pope, who decided his legate had been too harsh and allowed the archbishop to resume his post on certain conditions. Bruno was stuck in a very precarious position within the diocese. Some of the other complainants reconciled with the bishop out of fear, but Bruno maintained his stance with integrity. The pattern of abuse, complaint, trial, and reconciliation went on for three more years before Gregory finally removed Manassès.

Upon Manassès's departure, Bruno was asked to serve as the next archbishop, but to the disappointment of many, Bruno declined. During his four years of administrative limbo, he had begun to feel God nudgeing him in the direction of greater solitude and contemplation, away from the intrigue of ecclesial politics. Bruno chose to respond in fidelity to that inner voice.

In 1081, Bruno departed from Reims to affiliate with a Benedictine monastery. But after a few years, Bruno again felt that inner nudge, beckoning him toward even greater solitude. Along with several fellow monks, he headed south toward Grenoble. The local bishop, Hugh, welcomed Bruno warmly and helped him identify an isolated valley within the Alps called Chartreuse, where the tiny band might be able to build individual log cabins around a common chapel. Because of their unique location, they came to be called the Carthusians. It seems important to note, however, that the original band had no intention of founding a new religious order or recruiting others to join them. Indeed, their only regular visitor was Hugh, who so often sought refuge in their midst that Bruno finally had to urge him: "Go! Go to your sheep! And do what you are obliged to do!"

Little did Bruno know that his words to Hugh would soon boomerang. While Bruno was enjoying newfound peace in the silence of the Alps, the wider Church plunged into grave turmoil. Gregory died, and the German emperor Henry IV—one of the reform's greatest opponents—immediately circumvented proper channels for electing a new pope, instead installing his own choice, a deposed archbishop named Guibert. When a legitimate pope was subsequently elected, that new pope was so frightened of Henry and Guibert that he spent the remainder of his life hiding in a monastery. But the following pope, a former student of Bruno's who took the name Urban II, was determined to continue the reform by appointing administrators capable of enforcing Gregorian policies.

Early in 1090, Bruno received a letter from Urban requesting his presence in Rome to serve in the pope's inner circle of councilors. Bruno was undone. He had already spent a quarter of a century in church administration and did not aspire to return. The call to solitude had felt so clear and authentic. And yet, he could not ignore Urban's request. Bruno entrusted the tiny

Carthusian community to the leadership of his friend Landuino and headed back to Rome that spring.

By summer, Henry and Guibert had waged an attack on the city, and Urban's entire papal court was forced to seek refuge in Calabria, a region of southern Italy where several Norman princes offered them protection. Bruno asked for permission to return to Chartreuse. Urban instead asked Bruno to serve the very delicate post of archbishop in Reggio. Over many conversations, the two reached a compromise that met at least some of the interests of each party. Bruno would stay in Calabria so as to be accessible to the pope for counsel and support. In return, Urban would allow Bruno to establish a hermitage on the property of one of their Norman protectors, where he would be free to pursue a more contemplative life and not assume the role of bishop. In late 1091, Bruno established Saint Mary of La Torre hermitage alongside several other men interested in the new venture.

Bruno's final ten years were spent at Saint Mary's. He remained in contact with his original community through letters. "As regards myself," one letter reads, "know that what I desire most after God is to go to see you." Unfortunately, unsafe travel conditions created by Henry and Guibert never permitted such a visit before Bruno's peaceful death of old age in 1101.

Officially, Bruno is the patron saint of Calabria and those warding off demons, but we might also consider Bruno a patron for all administrators who are seeking to be faithful to the needs of God's people and the call of their own hearts at one and the same time. In Bruno, we meet a model of integrity—a man who always did what he felt was the right thing to do, while still remaining within the Church, in dialogue with Church leaders who sometimes saw things differently. Bruno teaches that one need not be strident while still being strong.

For **Reflection** *and* **Prayer**

1. What do you think the poet and philosopher John O'Donohue means when he says that "the only appropriate response to privilege is absolute integrity"? In what ways are you in a position of privilege?

2. Can you tell the story of a time when your work as an administrator invited you to greater integrity in your own life, and you changed your behavior?

3. Is there a situation in your administrative ministry in which what you say you believe and what you actually do need to be brought into greater harmony? How will you address this?

4. Is there a situation in which what your institution professes as a value and what it is actually doing need to be brought into greater harmony? What do you see to be your role in tending to the institution's angel?

5. What insight does the life of St. Bruno offer as you ponder the call to greater integrity?

O God,
In the opening words of scripture you said,
"Let there be light," and there was light.
Throughout the Bible, we see time and time again
that whatever you say comes to be.
You, O Lord, possess perfect integrity:
your word and your action are one and the same.
There is nothing incongruent between what you
    say and what you do.
But it is not so with me, O God.
The gap between what I advocate and what I
    actually do
is sometimes wide and deep.
May my work call me to ever-greater integrity, O
    Lord.

Open my eyes and my heart to the opportunities
for change and growth
that you continually place before me.
Amen.

Administration calls us to . . .

6. Humility

> What others think of us would be of little import did it not, when known, so deeply tinge what we think of ourselves.
>
> —George Santayana
> *Reason in Common Sense*

Administration has moments that make us aware of how much we have learned and grown over time in ministry. Tasks that a new employee might find difficult we suddenly realize have become very easy for us. Dilemmas others find perplexing and overwhelming we can resolve clearly and quickly. Those are good moments. We become conscious of the gifts we bring to our work and just how much knowledge we have managed to acquire. But let's face it; those are not the only kinds of moments that punctuate our days. Just as often, administration has moments that make us aware of our shortcomings and limitations. There are times in the office when we sit in front of good and holy and talented people and think, "Who am I to be giving them advice? I don't know the answer any more than they do," or, "Who am I to be making judgments about which candidate would be the better hire? I'm not God!" There are times we find ourselves at important meetings, being asked questions we don't know the answers to, looking at financial reports we don't really understand. There are times we lose our temper, miss a deadline, accidentally bypass a step in the chain of command, or blow a project. And then we are supposed to write an annual performance evaluation for another? Hello, Splinter, this is Plank speaking.

Researchers at the Harvard Negotiation Project note that one of the factors making these latter moments so difficult is that they evoke within us "an identity quake." Each of us, they observe, would like to think of ourselves as good, competent, and loveable. But moments such as these throw one or more of those identities into question. We find ourselves to be not as good, not as competent, or not as loveable as we want to believe. At these times we often turn the blame on others or—equally as dangerous—on ourselves.

Brad Binau, a former pastor and now dean of a Lutheran seminary, has written about a heightened sense of shame among many administrators. Binau draws a distinction between guilt, which persons experience concerning actions they have done or not done, and shame, which persons experience unattached to particular actions. Beyond not doing enough, shame is the feeling of not being enough. Beyond the sense of doing wrong, shame is the sense of being wrong. Shame, he says, results from an impotence to alter things. In administration, it comes from having too much responsibility with too little power to actually effect a change. Shame has the potential to paralyze persons, making those who already feel overwhelmed by tasks even less able to deal with those tasks and thereby less effective in their positions.

But administration offers us options beyond becoming defensive: "It is your fault that I missed the deadline," or defenseless: "I must just not be any good at this job." Indeed, administration has the capacity to make us appropriately vulnerable, which is a wonderfully holy thing. First, administration helps us gather a more accurate, truthful picture of ourselves. It puts us in situations that we would not otherwise confront, allowing us to see how we handle certain kinds of demands and pressures. It is stressful enough that we can't manage to put on a good face week after week, month after month, without our true selves coming to the surface. We can try to hide our temper, our procrastination, our indecisiveness—or any number of other vices—for a while, but eventually, the work of administration will bring it to the surface; and you will know sides of yourself you wish were not there, certainly sides you wish others didn't know.

At that point, administration can offer a second gift: the opportunity to become comfortable with the true picture of yourself.

It turns out that none of us is as good, as competent, or as loveable as we would like to be, and if we don't expect ourselves to be perfect, then we are less likely to be disappointed when we do something imperfect or even really lame. Binau notes that in the sacrament of Baptism, we are asked to "renounce Satan and all his empty promises." One of those empty promises is that we can somehow do everything without error, that we can somehow meet all needs of all people at all times. If we know, for instance, that we are not totally competent in our jobs, when others present us with evidence of some incompetence, we are able to say, "You are right, it looks as if I did that wrong. I am still growing in my job. Thanks for pointing that out." Or, if we know that we are not perfectly good, we won't be surprised when others let us know we have offended them. "I didn't intend to hurt you," we can say, "but maybe I didn't choose my words as carefully as I should have. Can you let me know if you see me do it again?" Our identity may still be shaken, but the quake need not knock us to the ground. It is possible to not be a perfect administrator but still be a good-enough administrator, en route to becoming a better administrator.

The Christian tradition calls this kind of balanced, truthful sense of self "humility." Humility is not about putting oneself down or placing disproportionate focus on one's weaknesses. Humility is synonymous with being honest about oneself. It involves acknowledging those good, affirming moments in our day as well as the challenging, quaking ones. It requires knowing our gifts and strengths and successes and knowing our weaknesses and growing edges. It implies being willing to present the most accurate representation of oneself whenever possible, aware that there may be even more to our true selves that we have yet to learn.

Humility is essential to the Christian journey. Indeed, without humility none of the other virtues in this book will serve your spiritual life. It is a little difficult to explain why, but it has to do with the nature of God as Trinity. When we say that God is Trinity, we are saying that the very essence of God is *relationality* or *being-in-relationship*. To experience salvation—as discussed in the introduction of this book—implies a sharing in the fullness of the life God dreams for us: God's very own life, Trinitarian life, relational life. If we cannot be honest and truthful about ourselves, there is no way that we can be in honest and truthful relationships with others, and consequently there is no way that we can participate in God's Trinitarian life. Belief in the Trinity is the foundation of our faith. We cannot live that belief without humility.

If, through the work of administration, we are able to shake false pictures of self, comfortably wear our own face before others, and say with confidence, "Now I am myself," then administration will have given us the cornerstone of the spiritual life, the greatest gift of all.

Companion for the Journey: **Martha**

Feast: **July 29**

Precious little is known of St. Martha. There exists no record of when she was born or when she died. We have little evidence of her social class or how she spent her days. And yet, Christian tradition strongly suggests that she was a treasured friend of Jesus and a highly significant figure in the early Church.

There are two passages in the canonical gospels that make mention of Martha. The first, and perhaps best known, is found in Luke 10:38–42. Martha welcomes Jesus into her home and offers him hospitality.

She busies herself with serving Jesus and perhaps his cadre of disciples as well, while her sister, Mary, sits at Jesus' feet and listens to him speak. Martha complains to Jesus, but instead of nudging Mary into action, he replies, "Martha, Martha, you are anxious and worried about many things." Jesus then tells her that "only a few things are needed" or, depending on the translation, "only one thing" and that "Mary has chosen the better part." Talk about unwelcome self-knowledge!

Luke's story clearly was a favorite in the early Church, as its frequent appearance in patristic homilies illustrates. It was applied in many different situations to teach many different lessons, but often around the nature of hospitality. Martha is a generous host who wants to make sure her guest is honored and well fed, yet her efforts to make sure everything is just so frazzle her. One gets the sense that she has eagerly anticipated the arrival of Jesus, but now that he is finally here, she is not able to enjoy a moment of his company. Martha's dilemma parallels that of many contemporary administrators who spend so much time preparing and serving others that they are not much able to enjoy the events they organize. Jesus' comment to Martha should be interpreted as a comforting one for administrators: it is not necessary to prepare so many "dishes" to serve; what is more important is being present to those we want to serve.

Many scripture scholars suspect, however, that Luke's verses are about much more than a single dinner in the home of Martha and Mary. The choice of the verb "serve" to describe Martha's action is laden with significance. This verb—in Greek *diakonia*—is the same one that is often used to describe Jesus' ministry (e.g., "I have come not to be served but to serve"). It is also used repeatedly to describe ministers in the early Church, especially those who serve at table in the first house churches. It seems possible that Martha may have been a leader in one of these, and her busyness in the Lukan episode refers not so much to a particular meal, but to all of the troubles she experienced in trying to keep up with the needs of the fledgling Christian community. Again, the voice of Jesus in the situation is not a critique of service (this is what Jesus teaches and models after all) but rather a concern about the anxiety and worry the exercise of leadership is causing in Martha. Perhaps Jesus is saying that the one thing needed in leaders is the capacity to first sit down and listen for a while, rather than engage in endless activity.

Facets of Martha's personality are subtly reconfirmed in the other scripture passage in which she appears, John 11:1–12:8. This passage begins with Martha and Mary sending a message to Jesus that their brother, Lazarus, is ill. By the time Jesus arrives, Lazarus has died and been buried. In John, as in Luke,

Martha is the first character on the scene, coming out to greet and welcome Jesus as he approaches their town. She is also again the pragmatic and straightforward sister. When Jesus commands that the stone be removed from Lazarus's grave, Martha points out, "Lord, there will be a stench; he has been dead four days." After Lazarus's raising, the story picks up again in the siblings' home, where Martha is once again identified as serving at table, while Jesus and the others recline. Both the Lukan and Johannine accounts could be seen as presenting Martha in a slightly unflattering light. She doesn't seem to understand Jesus' actions at first. And yet, one has to ask: how do we even know these stories unless Martha herself was the source? We sense the humility of this early Christian leader who freely shared her foibles and misunderstandings in the context of sharing the Good News with others.

Noncanonical texts from the first five centuries flesh out the Church's memory of Martha further. One text from the third century names Martha as an apostle and places her along with Mary at the Last Supper. A Greek fourth-century text mentions Martha as "serving the many and working hard." An ancient Coptic prayer book includes a list of the twelve male apostles followed by the names of eleven women, each of whom bears a descriptor. Martha is described as "a joyous servant" and then in a later place as "the breath of discretion."

Here, however, the already sketchy trajectory of Martha's life grows more faint. While her memory was clearly alive and influential among our earliest ancestors in the faith, no one knows what exactly happened to Martha later in life. A persistent hagiography places Martha, Mary, and Lazarus on a rudderless boat blown by the Holy Spirit in the direction of southern France, where they became missionaries.

Many of the later allusions to Martha in Church history continue to emphasize her down-to-earth pragmatism as an important counterbalance to some of Christianity's more esoteric pursuits. The German mystic Meister Eckhart preached Martha as the sister who was well grounded and able to engage in compassionate action, while Mary was still in an earlier learning phase. When Martha approaches Jesus about nudging Mary toward the kitchen, Eckhart says she is asking Jesus to show Mary how action and contemplation can come together in service, but Jesus tells Martha she needs to be patient. Mary is not as advanced in the spiritual journey as Martha and needs more quiet time still.

Such reinterpretations of Martha's story over time witness to a Church that is ever struggling, like Martha, to find the right balance between service and prayer, between actively addressing the needs of a hungry world and resting in the goodness of God. They remind us that while Mary may have "chosen the better part," the fullness of the Body of Christ is made up of many parts, and it needs the likes of Martha as well as Mary to fulfill its vocation in the world. In the midst of the struggle, Martha becomes a wonderful spiritual companion for those whose part in the Body of Christ often involves the mundane and worldly. She empathizes with an inner compulsion that drives some of us to try to fix things. She understands what is it like to get stuck with the heavy lifting, when no one else even seems to notice what needs to be done. At the same time, she receives Jesus' words as truth she needs to ponder. She knows the regret of having missed the party she hosted, and she steers us toward greater patience with others and greater kindness toward ourselves. She agrees there is a time to sit, though she is still trying to figure out just when that might be.

For Reflection *and* Prayer

1. What are the kinds of events in your administrative work that evoke "identity quakes"? Which is the greater temptation for you in moments of "identity quake"—blaming others or blaming yourself?

2. Can you tell the story of a time when you were able to learn something new about yourself in the course

of your administrative ministry? What has been the fruit of this discovery?

3. Is there a situation in your current administrative ministry in which you might need to be more honest with yourself? How can you do so?

4. What clues does the story of St. Martha offer in regard to practicing humility? How will you try to incorporate these into your work?

Most Holy Trinity,
You invite me to share in your divine, wholly relational life.
Teach me to be more vulnerable and honest in all my relationships,
beginning with my relationship to myself.
Hold before me a mirror that I might see myself for who I truly am,
gifted and challenged, virtuous and sinful, strong and weak,
all at the same time.
This is the person that you love and accept.
Teach me to love and accept myself as well.
Amen.

Administration calls us to . . .

7. Courage

> "I wish it need not have happened in my time," said Frodo. "So do I," said Gandalf, "and so do all who live to see such times. But that is not for them to decide. All we have to decide is what to do with the time that is given us."
>
> —J. R. R. Tolkien
> *The Lord of the Rings*

A commonly repeated joke tells of a mother coming in to wake her son for school. The son pulls the sheets over his head and whines, "I don't want to go."

"Give me three good reasons why you shouldn't go to school," the mother replies.

"I don't like school," he complains. "They give you too much work. Plus, all the kids make fun of me and are mean to me. Give me three good reasons why I should have to get out of bed!"

"I will," she retorts. "Number one, the sun is up; two, the bus is coming; and three, *you are the principal*."

This is how it is sometimes, isn't it? We wake up to find ourselves in roles of significant responsibility without quite knowing how it happened. It seems as if it was just yesterday we graduated from school. Now, our work asks us to tackle issues that we don't quite know how to handle—issues that take us far beyond our comfort zones. It can be rather overwhelming. Queasiness settles in the gut: "This job requires someone bigger than me. Someone older. Someone wiser. Surely, grown-ups used to be smarter when we were kids!"

At this point, the virtue of humility in the administrator must find its complement in the virtue of courage or fortitude. No, we don't know everything we wish we knew. No, we are not perfect. No, we don't feel worthy to make recommendations that will affect others' lives. But we also have to act. We have to ask difficult questions. We have to make and implement unpopular decisions. We have to confront the conflict. We have to cultivate an ability to respond that matches our responsibility.

Often as an administrator, I find myself in situations with students and colleagues that I would very much prefer to avoid. I fear that I do not have the wisdom or experience that I should to be dealing with the issues at hand. Nevertheless, there they are and here I am. I *do* have enough experience to know that no matter how badly I might botch things up through direct confrontation, it will be better than how badly I would botch things up by not directly confronting. In the words of Helen Keller: "Avoiding danger is no safer in the long run than outright exposure. The fearful are caught as often as the bold." In the moment, however, this is not much of a consolation.

In such times, I find that I must rely, not on my own inner resources, but on what I have come to call "the grace of the role." The liturgical calendar of the Catholic Church is filled with celebrations in honor of holy persons, but once a year we engage in the unusual tradition of celebrating a *chair*—the Chair of St. Peter. To outsiders, it sounds very odd to have a feast dedicated to a piece of furniture. But of course we are not honoring a historical artifact so much as the role of the person who sits in that chair.

Throughout history, many different people have held the role of bishop of Rome, some extremely saintly and others dreadful scoundrels. But what we trust is that the role itself brings a certain grace with it to compensate for the shortcomings of its current occupant. I am not saying that my "chair" merits comparison with that of Peter's, but I do suspect that there is a certain grace that comes with being appointed to fulfill a needed role in a community. And it helps in difficult moments to remember that someone has asked me to serve in this capacity and appointed me to carry out the task. There may be someone better out there, but that person is not sitting in the chair right now, and the work still needs to be done. I have to trust that the gap between me and what the role requires will be filled by the Holy Spirit.

In Paul's Second Letter to Timothy, there is a wonderful line in which Paul encourages Timothy to "stir into flame" the gift of God that Paul knows is within his disciple, reminding him that "the Spirit God has given us is no cowardly spirit, but rather one that makes us strong, loving, and wise" (2 Tm 1:6–7). Whenever I hear these words, I remember my son at age three, standing before the door of his preschool classroom, tears rolling down his face. The days for bringing your mom with you into the room were now over. He needed to go in by himself, but it was a frightening venture. I knelt down next to him and told him that I would give him a blessing to help stir into flame the courage that was inside him. At the end, he mumbled a question. I thought he asked, "Is Gabby with me now?" Gabby was a little girl from the neighborhood that he knew. "Yes!" I pointed inside the door, "She is right over there.

See?" "No!" he shouted. "Is *God* with me now?" "Oh, yes, sweetheart. God is with you." He wiped his nose on his shirtsleeve, dried his eyes, stood up straight, and pulled down his shirttail. Then, without another word, he turned around and walked into the classroom.

When I am anxious or overwhelmed in my job, I remember my son and try to imitate what I saw him do that day—minus the nose on the shirtsleeve. I recall that, in the end, my feeling confident or competent is far less important than knowing God goes with me into the encounter. Learning to trust that the grace of the role is real—God *will* be there—cultivates within the administrator, over time, genuine courage.

While there are many definitions of courage available, none capture the essence of the virtue better than the words of Dominican Marie-Joseph Lagrange, founder and administrator of the *École Biblique* in Jerusalem, who said of his own controversial work, "Knowingly and prudently, I stuck my hand into the fire." Lagrange's quip encapsulates the paradox that is courage—a blend of intentionality and foolhardiness as well as the foresight to see what could happen and the willingness to risk it anyway. The good news, I've discovered, is that the more often one sticks one's hand into the fire, the tougher one's skin becomes. The fire can still blaze intensely, but we feel the heat less. The fire becomes less frightening. Like the famed Shadrach,

Meshach, and Abednego from the book of Daniel, we become able to live in the furnace that is our life without trying to escape. We become able to praise God no matter what the circumstances.

Companion for the Journey: **Ambrose**

Feast: **December 7**

When we consider models of what it might look like to "knowingly and prudently" stick one's hand into the fire, we need look no further than the example of Ambrose of Milan—a man whose constant courage has long captivated scholars of Church history.

Ambrose was born around AD 339 in Trier, an ancient Roman city in what is now Germany. His father was the prefect of the region. Ambrose followed in his father's footsteps, anticipating a career in law and government. But desiring to be closer to the political pulse of the empire, he moved to Milan in northern Italy. In the year 370, he was appointed governor of the region by the Western Roman emperor Valentinian I.

The city of Milan was rich in religious diversity, home to Jews, traditional Roman worshipers, and various strains of Christianity. The Christians primarily fell within two camps—the Nicenes, who held that Jesus was one with and equal to God the Father, and the Arians, who argued that Jesus was divine but subordinate to the Father. Animosity between the two groups ran deep and dangerous.

When the bishop of Milan died in 374, the city found itself on the precipice of disaster. Given the stature of the city within the empire, both Nicene and Arian Christians had a vested interest in making sure the next bishop supported their views. In other areas around the empire, similar episcopal elections had sparked violence and riots. As governor, Ambrose did not want to see the Milan election devolve into citywide chaos and decided to be present during the process to ensure order. Much to his surprise, upon arriving at the gathering he heard his own name surface as a candidate who would be acceptable to both camps. Soon the crowds began chanting their approval.

There were several problems with this arrangement. First, Ambrose did not want the job and employed a variety of tactics to avoid assuming the role—all to no avail. (Resistance appears to be a common trope in Christian literature; no one who actually wants a leadership role is perceived to be worthy of it.) Second, and more significant, Ambrose was not a Christian. Ambrose clearly was sympathetic to Christianity at the time of his election, but he had never been baptized and, hence, had never attended Christian liturgy. In order to become bishop, Ambrose had to be baptized and then ordained within a one-week period.

Despite his initial resistance, Ambrose did embrace his new role with sincere commitment. He sold his personal possessions. He became a serious scholar of scripture and devoted himself to the ministry of preaching. Among Ambrose's most treasured legacies to the Church are a collection of baptismal Easter homilies that he preached and a series of hymns, with haunting Eastern melodies that linger in the mind.

For the purposes of this book, however, it is most important to consider the significant part that administration played in Ambrose's ministry. As bishop of Milan, Ambrose had frequent contact with both the Western and Eastern Roman emperors, giving his voice disproportionate weight among the bishops of his day.

Upon the death of his former sponsor, Valentinian I, Ambrose quickly established relations with the new Western Roman emperor, Gratian. Ambrose produced a series of texts called *De Fide*, in which he explained and advocated the Nicene Christian faith for Gratian. He urged Gratian to suppress traditional Roman worship. Such actions made Gratian unpopular with certain contingencies within the empire, leading to a revolt and ultimately to the assassination of Gratian in 383.

Valentinian II—son of Valentinian I and younger brother of Gratian—was only a boy when entrusted with the role of emperor. His mother, Justina, an Arian supporter, played a major role in shaping the policies of his governance, but Ambrose remained active in asserting his own Nicene leanings. When Valentinian II asked to use Ambrose's cathedral for Arian Easter services, Ambrose refused, creating a tense standoff between Ambrose's parishioners and the emperor's troops. Eventually, Valentinian backed away.

Upon the early death of Valentinian II at the age of twenty-one, the Eastern Roman emperor Theodosius assumed governance of the West, and Ambrose had a new leader with whom to contend. Ambrose and Theodosius shared many common causes. Both favored Nicene beliefs and sought the end of traditional Roman religion. But unlike the previous two Western Roman emperors, Theodosius was uninterested in Ambrose's advisory services. Ambrose's efforts at building a relationship with the emperor were damaged by his insistence that the emperor sit among the laity when visiting Ambrose's church in Milan, rather than with the clergy near the altar. And they were further injured by Ambrose's undesired interference in an issue regarding the destruction of a synagogue by a mob of unruly Christians and their bishop in Callinicum, a city at great distance from Milan, in what would now be Iraq. While the emperor backed away from penalizing the Callinicum Christians because of Ambrose's insistence, it is also likely that the incident caused Ambrose to become an increasingly peripheral voice in the emperor's circle.

Ambrose's rocky relationship with Theodosius arrived at a certain détente in 390, after a regrettable event in the Greek city of Thessalonica. Following the arrest of a popular charioteer, the people of the town advanced upon the prison to set him free, killing a number of the emperor's men in the process. The Roman army was given permission by the emperor to punish the offenders, but they did so in such a disproportionate manner that the whole empire was shocked. Records indicate that as many as 7,000 people were slaughtered.

When the emperor arrived in Milan after news of this event had spread, Ambrose refused to come greet him. Theodosius was in a very difficult situation, having wanted to establish himself as a temperate and tolerant ruler. It seems likely that he did not order the massacre but that he was unable to admit publicly that he did not have control of his troops. In a confidential letter, Ambrose proposed to Theodosius a process of reconciliation facilitated by the Church in Milan. Theodosius would admit his guilt and do penance, and Ambrose would publicly forgive him, welcoming him back into the assembly of the faithful. It was the first time that such a public reconciliation had been tried between a government leader and the Church, and it worked well, helping Theodosius to regain credibility among the people and helping Ambrose to keep the episcopacy a vital voice in the emperor's ear. At the end of his life, Theodosius is reported to have claimed, "I know of no bishop worthy of the name, except Ambrose."

In the mid-380s, Ambrose recorded many of the insights he had gleaned from his experience in a text called *De Officiis*, or "On Duty." In it, he outlined the high standards he expected for the Church's ministers. As a minister, one is always in the public eye, he notes. One must be impartial, constantly polite, careful in one's speech and dress, even conscious of one's gait. Because the minister's role set one apart from the general populace, Ambrose thought it very important that ministers form strong friendships with one another. "Preserve, my sons, the friendship into which you have entered with the brothers," he writes. "For it is the solace of this life for you to have someone to whom you may open your heart, with whom you may share private things, and to whom you may entrust your innermost secret. You then have in place a faithful man who will rejoice with you when things go well, suffer with you in times of sorrow, and encourage you when you are attacked."

It remains unknown who might have played such a role in Ambrose's life. Descriptions paint him as a competent, intelligent, professional person, but aloof and difficult to know. His writings portray someone who was probably a challenge to love. Ambrose was very sure of the righteousness of his causes, sometimes creating "straw men" of his opponents. His tone could be hectoring, his methods abrasive. And yet, across the ages, people have been impressed by Ambrose's courage and tenacity before power. He was outspoken, even when the situations he faced seemed beyond his influence.

Ambrose died in 397 after the journey to install a fellow bishop proved too grave a strain on his health. Ambrose told his clergy that God had made known to him that he would only be with them until Easter. Always true to his word, Ambrose died on Holy Saturday. As he was carried from the Vigil service through the city to his tomb, throngs pressed forward to touch him. His episcopacy ended just as it had begun, in the midst of clamoring crowds crying out his name.

For **Reflection** *and* **Prayer**

1. How do you balance humility and courage in your administrative ministry? How do you know when to say, "I'm not sure I can do this; I need help," versus the moment to say, "I'm not sure I can do this, but I need to act"?

2. Can you tell the story of a time when you stirred into flame the Spirit that lives within you in order to confront a difficult challenge?

3. Is there a situation in your administrative ministry at present where the spirit of courage may need to be stirred into action again? A situation that you have been avoiding that you know you need to address? How will you begin to address this?

4. What insights does the life of St. Ambrose offer to you regarding the righteous practice of courage? How can you use these to become a better administrator?

Spirit of God,
My work will confront me with difficult situations
and challenges
that I would rather not encounter.
Such situations lead me to doubt whether I have
what it takes
to serve you well in this role.
They make me wonder whether someone else
might not do a better job.
And yet, here I am.

Spiral and swirl within me now to rouse the hidden strengths
that lie deepest at my core—strengths that come from you,
but that I rarely remember to stir into flame.
Arouse perseverance to work through obstacles.
Arouse renewed determination.
Arouse boldness in the face of adversity.
Arouse courage.
Yes, my Lord, arouse courage.
Amen.

Administration calls us to . . .

8. Reflection

You are going to spend your life dealing with the ordinary work
of caring for the sick and dying,
disputes between people who should know better,
the failure of marriages,
the child or youth who has done something really stupid,
the celebration of a life of someone you do not like,
questions of whether you still need an 8 o'clock service
for those who will not let go of Rite 1.
In short, you are going to live in ordinary time,
undramatic time,
in which your life will seem to dribble out one grain of sand at a time.

But you will know where you are.
You are in the time God has made possible,
Kingdom time,
and the work you do is the peace of God.

—Stanley Hauerwas
"Ordinary Time: A Tribute to Rowan Williams"

"Evaluation" and "assessment" are buzzwords that appear frequently in administrative circles. Accrediting agencies, grant foundations, potential donors—all want assurance that our students are learning, our clients served, our sick healed, our money appropriately stewarded, and our policies effectively kept. As part of their work, administrators are constantly being asked to collect and review data assessing the strengths and weaknesses of programs, persons, and processes.

Sometimes it can feel unnecessarily time consuming to always be looking back at the dribbles of ordinary tasks in ordinary times, asking critical questions, tinkering, and revising. Can't we ever leave good enough alone? Isn't anecdotal evidence sufficient? I know it worked. Why do I need a survey to tell me? And sometimes, the sharp eye developed through repeated assessment activity can actually become a hindrance to spiritual growth. I remember being at Mass many years ago while on vacation with my husband, who is an experienced liturgist. Sitting in silence after receiving Communion, he repeatedly leaned over and whispered commentary on how the parish we were visiting could rearrange the Communion lines for a more efficient flow. "Could we just pray?" I asked. "This is not our problem." Yet, a short time later, I found myself part of a small faith-group process in which I neglected to actually participate because I was too busy mentally evaluating the process itself and the skill of the facilitator. Once the critical eye has been turned on, it can be difficult to locate the off switch.

At the same time, it must be acknowledged that an ongoing habit of gathering data and reflecting upon it has the potential to foster real growth. In a culture that is predominantly future oriented—always looking forward—our work as administrators challenges us to look back and test whether our good intentions actually produced the impact for which we hoped. We say our graduates are able to do certain things. Can they? We write that the grant funds will produce specific results. Have they? In a furiously busy world always ready to leap into the next great adventure, our work forces us to pause and see what we can learn from where we have been.

Anthony de Mello, S.J., tells the story of leading a workshop after which another priest approached him and said, "I've been a priest now for fifty years. I used to say that I had fifty years' experience in ministry. Now I understand that I only have one year's worth of experience, repeated fifty times." De Mello praised the insight and humility of this man. How difficult it is to acknowledge the truth that we enter into patterns of reacting, in which we simply do the same thing over and over again, never learning from what we are doing so as to make needed changes in our behavior! Nor do we learn, many times, to savor and reflect on what is going right and to discover the "Kingdom time" right in our midst.

If we are sincerely engaged, the practice of ongoing reflection, assessment, and evaluation that administration demands of us makes it difficult to miss the learning that experiences offer. Assessment opens us up to feedback and looking at things from different points of view. Like the age-old practice of examination of conscience, assessment forces us to grow in awareness of our motivations, our decisions, and the effects of our actions. It gradually nurtures within us a permanent attitude of curiosity and wonder, so that we find ourselves constantly asking questions about where we've been, why, and where we are going. Repetitive patterns begin to stand out, and we see connections we hadn't before.

Perhaps the night sky offers the best analogy for the promise of reflection. Some people look up at the night sky and see beautiful but isolated points of light. Others, who spend a long time with the night sky, start to see not points but pictures. They begin to perceive invisible lines that connect the stars one to the other—relationships between the celestial bodies that the casual observer is never privileged to glimpse. Different persons will connect the dots in different ways and hence see different pictures. But those who look long enough will witness the entire sky become a canvas—an immense, living, changing work of art with dancing, shifting lines, even as the points of light remain fixed.

So it is in institutions. Some people will look at the history of an organization and see isolated events scattered across the expanse of time. But those charged with reflecting on these events begin to see constellations—relationships between the moments that others might miss. They see patterns and bigger pictures that knit the various facets of an institution's life together. This capacity to see hidden connections often emerges quite slowly. As the novelist Zora Neale Hurston once noted, "There are years that ask questions and years that answer them." We won't be able to glean all that is to be gleaned in a matter of weeks. But when we practice the kind of reflection administration requires over a long period of time, it wires the brain in such a way that we will see things others can't, further nourishing that breadth of vision discussed in the first chapter.

So far I have spoken primarily about how the kind of reflection administration cultivates can help us become better administrators and our institutions better institutions, but it seems important to mention that when a reflective mentality permeates our work, it naturally begins to permeate our personal life as well. When we practice reflection repeatedly, we become reflective people—not just during office hours, but at home, in civic discourse, in the shopping mall. I remember that about five years into my job, I suddenly became aware that I was moving through life in a different way than I had before I was an administrator. I was slower to jump to conclusions, more capable of standing back and analyzing a situation, more intentional about asking questions before acting. I made fewer impulsive decisions and took the time to consult more widely and ruminate for a bit. Administration had formed me not to react but to respond.

This overall quality of reflectiveness seems to me a critical resource for the spiritual life. Unless we can slow down enough to consider the trajectory and impact of our actions, we will never become aware of areas where ongoing conversion might be needed. We will fail to hear that still, small voice of God strengthening and confirming our present course or nudging us in a new life direction. I am not sure I would push the matter as far as Socrates or Thoreau, who asserted that the unreflective life is not worth living, but I can confirm that the unreflective life is a life not fully lived—a life of missed opportunity. We learn and develop as persons only through the process of reflection. Fortunately for us, our work continues to offer many occasions to practice.

Companion for the Journey: **Joseph Mukasa Balikuddembe**

Feast: **June 3**

The kingdom of Buganda that Joseph Mukasa knew as a child was one of the most prominent in all of African history. Under the leadership of Kabaka Muteesa I, the kingdom encompassed much of what is now southern Uganda, with a central city of 40,000 surrounding walled palace grounds nearly three miles in circumference. The palace compound was serviced by 500 pages, many of whom were destined to become Buganda's future chiefs. Born circa 1860 in a village along Lake Victoria, Mukasa became one of those pages at the age of fourteen. Recognized immediately for his attention to detail and leadership potential, he was assigned to the team responsible for the kabaka's private living quarters, eventually arising to be Kabaka Muteesa's personal assistant. Little could Mukasa have imagined, however, how his emergence within the palace court might coincide with significant changes in his people's history, requiring of him ongoing discernment and complex choices, which make him an intriguing model for the virtue of reflection highlighted in this chapter.

The kingdom of Buganda began receiving its first foreign visitors in the 1830s, when Arabian traders came seeking new markets and introducing Islam to the region. European explorers followed in the 1860s, leading to the arrival of English Protestant missionaries in 1877 and French Catholic missionaries in 1879. Muteesa welcomed each party and allowed them to teach their religion within his courts, carefully showing no group preference over the others in an attempt to balance the influence of their nations of origin. Mukasa first learned about Christianity in the kabaka's court, becoming a catechumen in 1880. He was baptized "Joseph" by the French White Fathers in 1882.

Muteesa's tolerance for the foreigners, however, was always tenuous, and only a few months after Mukasa was baptized, the White Fathers were forced to leave the area, and Catholicism was suppressed. The fledgling Catholic community elected Mukasa to serve as their leader in the priests' absence. With the assistance of several other pages, including his second-in-command, Charles Lwanga, Mukasa oversaw the four Catholic missions surrounding the court, continuing formation for catechumens and baptizing the dying. When the missionaries returned three years later, they found their 250 catechumens doubled and another 130 persons baptized.

It was during the missionaries' absence that Joseph Mukasa acquired his nickname, based on an episode in which he saved the kabaka from a large snake. In gratitude for his rescue, Muteesa granted Catholics the right to practice their faith freely again and allowed Mukasa to take from the palace treasury whatever was needed to meet the community's needs. The Catholic community took to calling Joseph "Balikuddembe"—meaning "they are at liberty"—in memory of the freedoms he won for them.

When Muteesa I died in 1884, he was succeeded by Mwanga II, the seventeen-year-old son of his tenth wife. Mwanga requested Joseph Mukasa to remain as his personal assistant and made him majordomo of the palace—administrator of all the pages and responsible for speaking in the kabaka's name. Perhaps out of respect for Mukasa, Mwanga allowed the Catholic missionaries to return to the court, but he maintained his father's hesitancy about the extent of their influence. Mwanga, like his father, observed that Christianity came to Buganda with strings attached. It was difficult to distinguish the religious, political, and economic intentions of the Europeans. And for new Christians such as Mukasa, how was one to remain loyal to one's homeland and its independence while at the same time embracing the religion of those who wanted to take it away? When missionaries critiqued certain African practices, was it a question of calling Bagandan life to conversion in Christ, or was it European cultural bias? How could one be both fully African and fully Christian?

These issues came to a head not long after the missionaries' return in July 1885. Joseph Mukasa had begun to experience tension with Mwanga over the kabaka's treatment of the pages. Traditionally, a kabaka could expect absolute obedience from his pages. For Mwanga, this included sexual favors. But Mukasa had become uncomfortable with Mwanga's expectations. As the overseer of the pages, he often sent the teens on various errands rather than releasing them to Mwanga. Mukasa was motivated in his actions by his Christian beliefs, but Mwanga accused him of being a European traitor within the palace.

In October, the simmering conflict boiled over when Mwanga ordered the death of an Anglican missionary bishop, James Hannington, who had entered into Buganda from the eastern side of the kingdom rather than the traditional southern route. Hannington was likely unaware that Bagandans considered such an approach very rude—akin to a robber sneaking in the backdoor rather than a guest appropriately arriving at the front. Joseph Mukasa, although he did not know Hannington, confronted Mwanga about his command that Hannington be killed and asked that his life be spared. The request was not honored.

Furious to be challenged on his authority, Mwanga revisited the topic two weeks later when he and Joseph Mukasa argued through an entire night about their differences. In the morning, Mukasa left and attended Mass at the Catholic mission, but he was then recalled by one of his pages back to the palace, where Mwanga accused him before others of plotting against the kingdom by conspiring with Europeans. Mwanga's chancellor, who appears to have had a longstanding grudge against Mukasa, ordered his immediate death.

Joseph Mukasa was taken from the palace to an area along the Nakivubo River, where he was beheaded and his remains burned before Mwanga repented of calling the trial and attempted to call off the execution. The date was November 15, 1885. Mukasa was twenty-five years old.

Mukasa's death could have intimidated the other young pages, diminishing their interest in the Christian life. It did not. The day of Mukasa's death, Lwanga and several other pages who had been catechumens went to the mission and requested Baptism. Over the course of the next several months, forty-five Christian pages, including Lwanga, were put to death, and still Christian enthusiasm did not wane. In 1887, Mwanga waged war against Britain unsuccessfully, and Buganda eventually became a protectorate of the British Empire.

Looking back, there are many things in the history of the African-European encounter that we wish could have gone otherwise. Hindsight, as they say, is twenty-twenty, and hopefully much has been learned. Joseph Mukasa, however, did not live in the history we desire but in the messy history that was. He lived in it with as much creativity as he could muster and more courage than most of us could dream. He reflected and assessed and made daily decisions in difficult situations—one star in a constellation much bigger than himself, but a luminous one.

For **Reflection** *and* **Prayer**

1. Has your experience of administration helped you to slow down and become more reflective as a person? Has it taught you to learn from your experiences?

2. Can you tell the story of a time when you became open to changing direction—either personally or institutionally—because of what you learned in the process of assessment?

3. Is there a situation in your administrative ministry at present in which God may be inviting you to become more reflective?

4. How does the life of St. Joseph Mukasa speak to you about living a life of reflection within complex circumstances?

O Lord,
The highway of life moves very quickly for me.
There is much I want to accomplish this week,
this month.
There are many places I need to go and many
people I want to see.
And yet, there are all sorts of speed bumps molded
into the road I travel,
asking me to slow down, to look around before
accelerating again.
Help me to welcome the moments when my job
demands I pause,
assess, and consider.
Help me, rather than seeing unnecessary
obstacles,
to embrace these opportunities to grow in
reflectiveness.

Open my eyes to all that these moments illumine
for me as an administrator
in this institution, and as a disciple in your reign.
Amen.

Administration calls us to . . .

9. Humor

"There is no use trying," said Alice. "One can't believe impossible things."

"I dare say you haven't much practice," said the Queen.

"When I was your age, I always did it for half an hour a day. Why sometimes, I've believed as many as six impossible things before breakfast."

—Lewis Carroll
Alice's Adventures in Wonderland

We all love to work with lighthearted people—people who can laugh and tell a good joke, who make the office a fun place to be. Yet, I struggled with whether to include humor as a chapter in this book. Certainly a good sense of humor is desirable, but the premise of the text has been to identify qualities that administration grows within us, and administration suffers a popular perception of making people less funny, not more. Most would suspect that if an administrator happens to be fun to be around, it is an accident of their personality, not that their job somehow nurtured joviality.

Yet, when I've done workshops with administrators around the nation, one of the qualities that they most frequently mention as a quality administration has cultivated within them is a sense of humor. I have come to realize that, as a group, we seem to know something about administration that the rest of the world does not, something we are good at keeping a secret: administrators find lots to laugh about.

Why? Believe it or not, the fields of philosophy, psychology, and biology have all devoted significant attention to the topic of humor and what makes us laugh. Most theories revolve around an experience of the absurd—something strikes us as incongruous with how things normally function in our world. Humans can have a variety of emotions around something not seeming quite right—anger, confusion, and so forth—but if the incongruity is perceived as benign, they find it humorous. A man charges us with a sword, and we are frightened. A rabbit charges us with a toothpick, and we snicker.

Currently, scientists tend to distinguish between two main types of humor: deprecation and elevation. In the first type, humor is a manifestation of the innate power struggle that exists in any human community. Plato actually described humor as a form of aggression. We take incongruities in human behavior and laugh at them as a way of taking pleasure in our own superiority. Sometimes this form of humor can be outright cruel—schoolyard teasing, the laughter of gossip—but many times it is very subtle and innocuous. We wouldn't find the Three Stooges or Charlie Chaplin movies funny if depreciating humor were not built into our genetic makeup. In the humor of elevation, the absurdity that life poses becomes a sort of riddle. When we are able to make sense of it, we enjoy a certain "aha" moment and feel the pleasure that comes from having worked something out for ourselves, a tiny burst of intellectual energy. Many humorous situations are a combination of deprecation and elevation.

I suspect the reason so many administrators describe administration as increasing their sense of humor is due to the perception that administration has placed them in an increased number of absurd situations. There is much in institutional life that seems perfectly clear to us as administrators but foggy to others. And in reverse, there is much that must appear logical to others but seems poppycock to us. Like Alice in the fictional Wonderland, most of us have been asked to believe a lot of "impossible things" in the course of our work, some days as many as six of them before we've managed to rinse our coffee mug. I cannot tell you the number of forms that I believe I had designed to be simple and straightforward but that came back to me a jumbled mess. At the same time, I would have a hard time counting the policies that I've been asked to implement that—from where I sit—seem utterly nonsensical. Whereas early in the ministry I might have gotten myself worked up or worried about the absurdity of things, experience has taught me that most things are more benign than what they appear and hence merit laughter more than angst. In the words of Thomas More, our companion for this chapter, "Happy is the person who can distinguish between a rock and a mountain; it avoids so many inconveniences."

At the same time, I feel that in lifting up humor as a spiritual fruit of administration, we have to give due credence to Plato and acknowledge that not all humor is spiritually enriching. Of course, most of the qualities discussed in this book are of a dual nature: there is a fine line between courage and foolishness, between humility and self-abasement, between generativity and compulsive activity. But the line between holy mirth and cynicism is often razor thin. I do believe that humor can be virtuous, but virtuous humor is not only the most difficult form of humor to develop; it is probably also the most difficult form of virtue to attain. Virtuous humor is a rare, mature trait.

In my own experience, the journey toward virtuous humor—and I would say I am only a beginner here—has required two initial acknowledgments. First, although I am classifying more things as benign by choosing to laugh at them rather than be upset by them, this may not always be the most honest classification. Laughing or making fun, as many psychologists have pointed out, can be a defensive mechanism—leading us to avoid acknowledging what we are really feeling, especially toward those things about which we feel negatively. In our humor, we encourage others around us to also laugh. Sometimes this can be a good thing—lightening up the mood so that everything is not taken so seriously. But sometimes in laughing we avoid addressing situations that probably should be addressed. In my case, humor can tend to mask anger, and generally not very well. A few years back, one of my colleagues helpfully said to me, "Ann, you want to make sure that your anger is like a coursing stream rather than a finely diffused mist." Frustration is best tackled candidly and with the source of the frustration, rather than first with everyone else in the office. But that is hard. It is easier to laugh with others who are not the source of my frustration, even if it means a large percentage of the office staff has now inhaled the mist of my anger.

Second, humor of deprecation has a limited value in the spiritual life. Sometimes self-deprecating humor can be a sign of true humility. It can indicate that persons feel comfortable in their own skin. As discussed earlier in this text, it is important that we know ourselves well enough to understand that we are not perfect, and that it is okay. Thomas More, for example, often used self-deprecating humor to great effect. But beyond small doses of self-deprecation, the humor of deprecation is at best morally neutral (i.e., watching Charlie Chaplin) and at worst morally reprehensible (i.e., taunting another person publicly). It doesn't really help one to grow personally in holiness, and it contributes, even if indirectly, to an unhealthy community life. The philosopher Rene Girard noted that humans tend to bond as communities through the process of scapegoating. They identify one person or group of persons as the problem, and then they create and strengthen relationships between themselves by talking about this one person or group. In essence, the recipe for group identity is "everyone minus one." Laughter and joking often play a role in the process. Although such jokes may be said "in good humor," communities established on the foundation of scapegoating can only maintain their life together by ongoing scapegoating.

Holy humor, by contrast, observes the very simple distinction of "laughing with" rather than "laughing at." Confronted by the same absurdities of institutional life, it chooses to respond in a different way—using humor to illuminate the absurdity rather than attack its source. I acknowledge that this is often a very fine line! But we gain some insight from Jesus' style of preaching in the gospels. Jesus frequently used humor to call people's attention to things in such a way that they would smile rather than feel embarrassed. Who really lights a candle and puts it under a basket? How preposterous! Who tries to do eye surgery while blinded by a plank? Silly, isn't it? Jesus found many of the institutions of his day absurd as well, but through humor, he did not galvanize persons against them so much as help them together to see the absurdity more clearly. The recipe for community in Jesus' cookbook was "everyone"—not "everyone minus one" but simply "everyone." His recipe for humor used the same ingredients.

Jesus also did not allow the absurdity of life to overshadow his fundamental belief in the goodness of being alive. From where he sat, every flower was decked out in all the finery of Solomon, and the hairs on each head were counted. Yes, there is the absurdity of evil and suffering and injustice and ineptitude, but there is also the absurdity of love and sunshine, not to mention the greatest absurdity: the absurdity of existence itself. Really, the whole universe is one great riddle—flaring forth from a speck smaller than a mustard seed—and the fact that any one of us is here at all should provide us with enough "aha" moments of delight to keep us rapt in laughter of elevation every day of our lives. Cynicism is the sign of too narrow a worldview, a constriction of vision that only notes the negative absurdities of life, whereas the most mature, holy administrators that I have known are people who have the capacity to also see and draw attention to the infinite positive absurdities of life.

Companion for the Journey: **Thomas More**

Feast: **June 22**

Few of the holy administrators introduced in this book ever sat for a portrait. And if they had, their portraits would likely look quite different than the one that St. Thomas More commissioned from the famed painter Hans Holbein in 1527. Many of the administrators portrayed in other chapters were celibate men and women. Many would be in religious habit. Many would be seated among the disadvantaged of society. In his portrait, by contrast, Thomas More is surrounded by a bustling household comprised of his father, wife, multiple grown children, and their spouses. He sits calmly in the midst of activity, as his family reads, converses, and gazes reflectively in various directions. A pet monkey crawls along the hem of his wife's dress. Books are strewn across the floor. All are clothed in noble garb. More wears around his neck the gold chain that identifies him as a high-ranking public servant and advisor to the king. Here is an administrator fully ensconced in the chaos of worldly life.

Thomas More was born around 1477, the son of a prominent lawyer. Thomas began legal studies at the age of sixteen. From a young age, he embodied a deep respect for the rule of law, treasuring the order and prosperity that England enjoyed because of its unique legal heritage rooted in the Magna Carta, which acknowledged that even a monarch's power had limits. But lest we think More to be a rather solemn sort, it is important we hear from his university friend, the great humanist scholar Erasmus, who describes Thomas as "always so pleased with a joke, that it might seem that jesting was the main object of his life. Gravity and dignity were never made for him."

As a young adult, More threw himself into family life. In 1505, he married sixteen-year-old Jane Colt, who bore three daughters and a son before dying, likely in childbirth, only six years into their marriage. Shortly thereafter Thomas wed Alice Middleton, herself a widow and eight years his senior. "Dame Alice," as she was known, was a straightforward woman who could match Thomas in wit and balance his love of the classics with a good dose of common sense. Thomas valued her as a debate partner and affectionately referred to her as the "Jolly Master-Woman." Alice and Thomas did not have any children of their own, but the More household continued to expand with the addition of Alice's daughter from her previous marriage and the guardianship of another young girl whose parents had died. More also enjoyed welcoming into his house a wide variety of animals: monkeys (as Holbein's picture highlights) but also ferrets, foxes, and weasels, with which he enjoyed surprising guests.

As More's household grew, so did his career as a lawyer and public servant. He was elected to Parliament and became active in the Merchant's Guild. For eight years, he served as chief legal counsel to the sheriff of London. He was appointed commissioner for sewers, working to increase public health along the Thames River. He oversaw the maintenance of the London Bridge. In each of these capacities, More's reputation for fairness and honesty, as well as good wit, only increased. In 1518, he consented to work in King Henry VIII's royal service.

More had known Henry VIII since boyhood since their families had a longstanding relationship. They enjoyed a lively friendship. And yet, from the beginning, Thomas had reservations about working directly under Henry, suspecting the monarch harbored a deep-seated lust for power that could come into conflict with Thomas's commitment to the rule of law. Later, More would advise Thomas Cromwell, a fellow member of the king's inner circle: "In the counsel you give His Grace, ever tell him what he *ought* to do, but never what he is *able* to do." Unfortunately, Henry proved more interested in testing the limits of what he was *able* to do.

The most troublesome example of Henry's drive for control involved his nearly twenty-year marriage to Catherine of Aragon—a marriage that had produced one daughter but no sons to inherit the throne. As Catherine passed her childbearing years, Henry became enchanted with one of her young maids-of-honor named Anne Boleyn. Henry desired to have his marriage to Catherine annulled so as to be able to marry Anne, but the pope at the time was—ironically—being held hostage by Catherine's cousin, the Holy Roman emperor Charles V. The situation was as politically dicey as it was morally reprehensible. Realizing that an annulment from the pope was unlikely, Henry decided that the capacity to make such a decision should be declared outside the pope's domain. Through a series of complicated legal maneuvers, Henry bullied the bishops and the Parliament to twist the laws of the land to conform to his wishes. He declared that Roman Catholic canon law held no sway in England and that the king of the country was the head of the Church in that country, as well as the head of the state.

Thomas was lord chancellor of England at the time Henry decided to break with Rome, a position of influence second only to the king. More's initial approach to the dilemma was to remain as a trusted and honest counselor to the king, consistent with his longstanding commitment to doing the best one can in the middle of the messiness of the world. As he stated at one point, "You must not abandon the ship in a storm because you cannot control the winds," but rather attempt to make things "as little bad as you can."

After three years as chancellor, however, More felt as if he could no longer remain in the role with integrity. Out of respect for the king's office and for the safety of his family, More committed to remain silent concerning his personal opinions on Henry's actions. More knew that, by English law, silence implied consent and that by refusing to speak on the matter, he was not doing anything that could be legally construed as treasonous. Unfortunately, Henry was not content with More's silence. In 1534, Henry mandated that More take an oath accepting the change of succession that would come with offspring born of Anne and Henry. When More would not, Henry had him imprisoned.

Various family members and friends from his past visited Thomas and tried to persuade him to take the oath, but he would not say anything he did not believe true.

Finally, Henry's collaborators arranged to have Richard Rich—a young lawyer interested in elevating his career—perjure himself on the witness stand at More's trial, claiming that More had explicitly denied Parliament's right to name Henry head of the Church of England. More was found guilty and sentenced to death.

In his final days, Thomas was greatly grieved by the pain his execution would cause his family, and yet he did not forsake his famed sense of humor. On approaching the scaffold, More pardoned the executioner and apologized that his neck was so short. Placing his head on the block, he asked to move his beard so that it would not be cut, since "it had not done anything to offend the king." More was beheaded July 6, 1535.

More's dilemma as the king's chief administrator is not terribly unlike the dilemmas that many administrators face, especially in relationship to their bosses and boards. When they see poor, even evil, decisions being made, should they stay and try to mitigate the bad effects, or should they go? Should they remain silent, or should they speak? Should they laugh it off, or take a stand? What is the best way to be faithful to the mission of the institution they serve? Thomas's life highlights the undesirable paradox that—in administration—the way to be most loyal to a leader is to tell the truth the leader doesn't want to hear. And the way to possess the greatest influence is to be willing to sacrifice all influence for the sake of living with integrity.

For **Reflection** *and* **Prayer**

1. Can you tell the story of a time when your work as an administrator evoked a new capacity to laugh at things in a way that you may not have previously?
2. Is the humor that you enjoy in your work right now primarily humor of deprecation or elevation?
3. Is there a situation in your administrative ministry at present where you may be challenged to stop getting upset and start laughing? Is there a situation where you may be challenged to stop laughing and try another approach?
4. What possibilities does the life of St. Thomas More illumine regarding the role of holy humor in administration?

God of Holy Mirth,
Over and over again in scripture we are told to wrap ourselves with joy.
"Rejoice!" your prophet Zechariah and your angel Gabriel announced.
"Rejoice!" your apostle Paul admonished. "Again, I say rejoice!"
Increase within me a sense of wondrous joy
at the riddle of the universe in which I live.
May the innate craziness and absurdity of my administrative tasks
unleash in me a capacity for holy laughter.
May I delight in all the ways you are at work in my midst,
especially those ways I neglect to acknowledge and take so easily for granted.
Amen.

Administration calls us to . . .

10. Forgiveness

> Forgiveness is the name of love practiced among people who love poorly.
>
> —Henri Nouwen
> *The Only Necessary Thing*

This chapter was not part of the outline for this book when I first sketched it out on a piece of scrap paper six years ago. The discovery of forgiveness as a prominent theme in administrative ministry is recent for me. Certainly I had spoken to lots of administrators who were frustrated within their institutions and had suffered at the hands of poor leaders or eccentric supervisors. Many of them told me stories that made me shake my head with indignation, "How can you stay?" And many times they would shrug their shoulders. Only recently have I learned to ask that question with greater sincerity, genuinely interested in what makes it possible for a person to remain in their work when they have witnessed fiscal mismanagement, questionable ethics, chronic unwillingness to address systemic problems, erratic decision making, yelling matches, utter ineptitude—you name it; these administrators had seen it all. I've become curious, "What is behind that shrug?"

This newfound curiosity, as you might suspect, has surfaced out of working through some markedly difficult events in my own institution—not anything distinctive or particularly embarrassing, but the same sort of stuff that every place faces in times of changing markets and demographics. When the sky is blue and the waters are calm, silt sinks to the bottom of the sea. It is there, but it doesn't really bother anyone snorkeling at the surface. When a storm moves through and the winds blow up and the sea becomes choppy, all that silt that usually lies quiet deep below is stirred, muddying the waters and making it difficult to see clearly where you want to go. My son recently showed me a poster that read, "When the winds of change blow hard enough, the most trivial of things can become deadly projectiles." If I remember correctly, it envisioned a stapler and canister of pencils whipping by. Funny, but I can kind of see how that could happen. In all honesty, I think that—given the nightly news of the past decade—most of us, whether we work in an ecclesial setting or a secular setting, would say we are a little less proud of our institutions than we were ten years ago. And probably most of us would admit we are a little less proud of ourselves, for how we've handled ourselves in the midst of crises. I, for one, would love to be able to take back any number of uncharitable things that have come out of my mouth.

And yet, many of these administrators to whom I've talked remain in their positions. "Why?" is an easy question to answer. Many need their jobs to support themselves, their families, and their religious communities. Furthermore, they believe in the mission of their institutions and the potential good that their institutions can do. But "How?" is a more difficult question, which brings us back to the shoulder shrug. How do you go back to work on a daily basis facing persons with whom you've exchanged harsh words? With whom you've vehemently disagreed? Persons you've sworn never to trust again? For many, the shrug of the shoulders, it turns out, is connected to forgiveness. Their work has taught them how to let go and move on.

First, let us dispel a few myths about forgiveness. Forgiveness is not the same as forgetting. Forgetting is not always possible, nor is it always wise. Forgetting can leave us unwittingly vulnerable to being hurt again by the same pattern of behavior. Forgiveness is also not a decision. It involves a decision to be open to forgiving (sometimes an hourly decision!), but in the end, forgiveness only comes about as a gift of God. We can and must will it, but God is the one who makes it happen. Forgiveness does not require the other party's apologizing. Of course, apologies go a long way, but God has the power to grant us the peace of forgiveness even without them. And finally, forgiveness is not the same thing as ignoring a situation, pretending it didn't happen, or sweeping it under the rug, saying, "It is okay," when it is not okay. Genuine forgiveness mandates honest conversation and confrontation. Can you imagine Jesus reappearing in the Upper Room on the night his tomb has been found empty pretending nothing had happened between him and those hiding there?

Rather, Jesus' resurrection visits give us a model for what forgiveness does look like. Jesus does not enter the room feigning everything is as it was before his friends betrayed him, denied him, abandoned him, and sold him for thirty pieces of silver. Nor does he unleash justifiable wrath upon them. Rather, he wishes them peace. Forgiveness is about wishing the best for the other, wishing that whatever would bring them the greatest life and light would happen for them. Now, sometimes the best thing that could happen to another person is that they find another job, that they hit rock bottom, even—in worst case scenarios—that they be put in prison. In most situations, that is not really ours to decide, but forgiveness is hoping that whatever "that" is does indeed happen. It means arriving at the freedom to genuinely will the best scenario for the good of the other.

An important feature of the Resurrection stories, I believe, is that Jesus' wounds remain exposed. In the case of Thomas, Jesus even invites his friend to touch them. Rising from the dead does not erase the crucifixion. It transforms it, robbing it of the power to predetermine the outcome of the relationship in the present. One of the best definitions of forgiveness might—interestingly—belong to comedian Lily Tomlin, who said that forgiveness is "letting go of every hope for a better past." Not to say that we can't hope for a better present or a better future, but we need to let the wounds be wounds and stop wishing we could go backward in time as if we could undo the past. The past is what it is, but we don't need to stay there.

How does forgiveness function in the workplace? Although the events that trigger frustration and anger vary widely, stories of moving toward being able to work together productively again share some common denominators. The first aid toward forgiveness seems to be *time*. In one of my worst months on the job, a mentor gave me a carved stone turtle to sit on top of the hard drive of my computer. It was supposed to remind me not to make decisions in haste or in anger, but to move slowly and intentionally. It is still sitting there, staring me in the face each morning. Time softens the edges of anger and sadness, making it easier to work with the emotions.

A second aid in the process is *recommitment to institutional mission*. In the moment of anger, we may not feel much allegiance to the institution itself, but then again, we don't work to serve the institution. We work to serve the mission for which the institution was founded. Remembering the mission gives us an impetus for beginning the reconciliation process. We may not always like all of the people with whom we work or the decisions that they make, but our desire to see the mission flourish motivates us to work through frustrations and disagreements.

It is generally easier to will the best for the institution's mission than it is to will the best toward individuals who have angered us. But a critical turning point is to decide that we *want* to will them the best, to decide to be open to the gift of forgiveness when God offers it rather than hold on to our injuries. Forgiveness is not usually a gift with which God is stingy. The problem isn't so much that God won't give us the grace to forgive but that we never even ask.

Finally, forgiveness is aided by *honesty and understanding*. Often it would be easier to be silent about our grievances, or (as discussed in the last chapter) to tell everyone except the persons with whom we are angry. But if we have the courage to express ourselves directly to the persons involved, naming our feelings, our perceptions, and our concerns and openly asking for theirs, we are likely to discover that the gift of forgiveness arrives more readily. Deep-rooted conflicts are unlikely to be resolved by such conversations. Indeed, many deep-rooted conflicts will never be resolved except by the grace of God. But that does not mean that we are free to ignore the difficult conversations.

Strangely, we must admit that God seems to be far more stingy with the gift of resolution than the gift of forgiveness. It would almost seem as if God has decided deep-rooted conflicts are to persist in the world, perhaps because such conflicts are a means of spiritual development for the human race—teaching us about God's design for difference and diversity, showing us how to be in fruitful relationship with one another even while still disagreeing. The choice to talk directly to those who anger and hurt us is definitely a more difficult path to travel than simple avoidance, but then again, it *is* holiness that we are pursuing here.

Before concluding this reflection, I want to acknowledge that I have focused here on what I have learned about forgiving others in the context of being an administrator, but I know there have been many times when others have been irritated and angered and frustrated with me. My job has not only given me practice in the art of forgiving; it has also provided me with many opportunities to experience being forgiven. One of my favorite proverbs from Egypt claims, "Many peace negotiations have broken down, not because no one came willing to forgive, but because no one came wanting to be forgiven." Perhaps even more challenging than initiating conversation with someone who has angered us is initiating conversation with someone whom we have angered. In a professional context—sometimes more than in a personal context—it can be really difficult to say, "I am sorry." And yet, how grateful I am to have had coworkers who were willing to move past an offense and continue to wish the best for me.

Companion for the Journey: **Mary MacKillop**

Feast: **August 8**

If you have ever felt trapped in an incredibly dysfunctional ministry environment, if you have ever looked around and wondered if everyone with whom you work is just a tinge crazy, or if you have ever been at a loss as to how to deal with the immense complexities of ecclesial politics, Mary MacKillop is the saint for you.

Mary's journey toward canonization was an unusual one. Indeed, there were periods in her life when such recognition seemed not only unlikely but impossible. Mary's perseverance and charity in the midst of deep struggle with the Church she loved make her a peculiarly striking model for the kind of forgiveness discussed in this chapter.

MacKillop was born near Melbourne, Australia, on January 15, 1842, the daughter of Scottish immigrants. As the oldest of eight children, Mary had to work at an early age in order to support the family. At eighteen, she moved to Penola, in rural southern Australia, to serve as governess for her young cousins.

MacKillop quickly recognized that children in the Outback had little access to education in general, much less faith formation. In addition to teaching her cousins, she soon found herself educating other children in the area. Her efforts caught the attention of Fr. Julian Woods, a local priest. Woods became MacKillop's spiritual director and nurtured her budding dream of dedicating her life entirely to God in ministry to the marginalized.

In 1866, twenty-four-year-old MacKillop opened the first Catholic school in Penola inside an old barn. The following year, Woods received permission from the nearby bishop of Adelaide, Laurence Sheil, to establish a new religious community called the Sisters of St.

Joseph of the Sacred Heart, or the Josephites. MacKillop was the first member and superior of the community. The rule emphasized poverty, trust in divine providence, and itinerancy. The sisters were not to live in convents but among the people in small clusters of two or three. Their practice was to follow farmers, railway workers, and miners as they moved for their work, living as they lived. Because of their brown habits and freedom to roam, they came to be popularly known as the Brown Joeys.

An able organizer, MacKillop quickly opened a number of institutions across southern Australia devoted to education, caring for orphans, sheltering the aged poor, and working with the incurably ill. MacKillop's efforts took her to Brisbane and then to Port Augusta. Both the need and the possibilities seemed endless.

Letters from Woods and the Josephite sisters around Adelaide, however, beckoned MacKillop back to where she had begun. An intractable conflict had broken out among Woods, the sisters, and the local clergy of the area. One source of conflict concerned a missionary priest in one of the parishes where the sisters served. While the details are difficult to ascertain, the sisters seem to have feared that the sexual abuse of minors was taking place. The priest was removed and sent back to Ireland, but a rift had been created between the sisters and diocesan officials. The rift was exacerbated by the behavior of two sisters who claimed to experience visions and by Woods who was prone to spiritual eccentricities of his own. MacKillop found herself defending Woods's rule for the congregation against the diocesan officials, who wanted to alter it so that the sisters were no longer under her leadership but that of the local parish priests. Simultaneously, she found herself confronting Woods about the harm his pietistic behavior was causing the congregation. Whenever Mary tried to raise her concerns about the two visionary sisters, he told her that she needed to rid herself of the temptation of doubt. When Mary tried to dismiss a mentally ill young woman from the community, Woods refused on the grounds of a local prophecy that the girl would become a great saint.

The tension climaxed upon Bishop Sheil's return from a long visit to Rome. Records from the period portray Sheil as a man of poor health suffering both from memory loss and alcohol abuse. Influenced by his disgruntled diocesan officials, Sheil announced a change in the structure of the Josephites and declared several sisters unfit for teaching. When MacKillop respectfully disagreed with the bishop over the changes, the bishop excommunicated her for insubordination. The excommunication lasted five months, during which time MacKillop was forbidden to speak with her sisters.

Mary's letters throughout this episode demonstrate remarkable charity: she urged her friends not to speak ill of the bishop. Mary actively sought opportunities to see the bishop and rectify the situation. She resisted publicizing what had taken place, although many in Adelaide were on her side. At the same time, she did not acquiesce to the bishop's demands regarding authority and organization within her congregation. On his deathbed, the bishop rescinded the excommunication, and the congregation reestablished itself with Mary as their leader. Lest one think that MacKillop's challenges with clergy were over, however, they had just begun.

To avoid future challenges to the community's rule, MacKillop decided to go to Rome and seek papal approval of the congregation so that it would no longer exist only at the whim of individual bishops. MacKillop was able to negotiate such that the rule was approved, naming the women superiors of the congregation to be the decision makers rather than diocesan leaders, but she agreed to changes in the community's practice of poverty. Her willingness to compromise on this matter with the Roman officials angered Woods, who thought she should have advocated for their original rule more vigorously. Woods broke off all official contact with MacKillop and the congregation, but in the years following this event, he frequently wrote letters to particular Josephite sisters complaining about Mary and trying to recruit them away into another religious congregation he wanted to establish. Again, Mary's correspondence during this period radiates both charity and honesty, never sacrificing one for the other. The balance is captured well in a comment from one of her letters regarding Woods's efforts to woo sisters away: "There is a painful want of straightforwardness in Fr. Woods' conduct which is a mystery to me in one so holy." Mary's repeated attempts to speak with Woods directly rather than through third parties were rebuffed until the final days before Woods's death in 1889. Nevertheless, upon his death, Mary raised funds for a chapel to memorialize him and wrote a very favorable biography of his life, in which there is little mention of the fifteen years of tension between them.

Mary's efforts to attain papal approval for her congregation evoked the ire of more than Woods, unfortunately. Her action also angered several Australian bishops who wanted more direct oversight of the Josephites' work in their dioceses. The new bishop of Adelaide, Bishop Reynolds, ordered an investigation to study the congregation and Mary's leadership. She was accused of drunkenness—based on willfully twisted medical records showing Mary had been prescribed several tablespoons of brandy to treat dysmenorrhea. She was also accused of financial mismanagement, despite detailed records demonstrating diocesan approval of all debts the congregation had incurred in their ministry. Through a complicated series of maneuvers, Mary was removed as superior of the congregation and replaced with another sister, Bernard Walsh, who was regarded by the Australian bishops as more pliable.

For the next decade, MacKillop served her congregation in a purely administrative role, as assistant to Walsh. Given how difficult it can be for a former leader and a new leader to serve side by side, the two seem to have worked hard to create good boundaries with each other. Yet, this new role was a very awkward one for Mary. Walsh had few of the leadership or administrative skills Mary possessed. She did not like to travel. She was not very savvy regarding civil or ecclesial politics. Mary struggled to figure out how to be honest and forthright with Walsh regarding decisions she found problematic, without looking as if she was undermining Walsh's authority.

Upon Walsh's sudden death in 1899, the sisters were for the first time allowed to elect their own leader per the dictates of their constitution. MacKillop was once again chosen as Mother General, but shortly thereafter she suffered a stroke that left her paralyzed on the right side. Undeterred, she learned to write left-handed so as to continue to communicate by letters with her sisters. She used a wheelchair to travel to them. The sisters reelected her to office in 1905, and she remained Mother General until her death in Sydney on August 8, 1909.

Mary's religious life had been filled with ecclesial tension, but in her final illness, Mary was visited by a steady stream of bishops and priests coming not to argue but to imbibe her holiness. One cardinal upon leaving commented, "Today, I believe I have assisted at the deathbed of a saint." Mary MacKillop's lifelong practice of forgiveness had made possible an atmosphere of true insight and reconciliation.

For Reflection *and* Prayer

1. What have you learned about the process of forgiveness from your experience in administration?

2. Can you tell the story of a time when you were able to forgive a supervisor or coworker? What made it possible? What did you learn about yourself?

3. Can you tell the story of a time when you have been forgiven by a supervisor or coworker? What made it possible? What did you learn about yourself?

4. Is there a situation in your administrative ministry at present where you may be challenged to let "go of every hope for a better past"?

5. What insights does the life of St. Mary MacKillop offer you concerning forgiveness in the workplace?

Jesus Christ,
You came to announce the reconciliation of the world to God.
Through your preaching and ministry, through your death and resurrection,
God has lavished upon this planet the healing power of forgiveness.
And yet, it is so hard to embrace this gift in my own life.
May I always desire forgiveness—both for those who have offended me
and from those whom I have offended.
May I fully cooperate with the reconciliation you proclaimed,
serving it rather than hindering it by my words and deeds.
Breathe your peace upon me and upon my coworkers.
Amen.

Administration calls us to . . .

11. Embrace Death

> When Christ calls a man, he bids him come and die.
>
> —Dietrich Bonhoeffer
> *The Cost of Discipleship*

To say that administration invites us to "embrace death" can sound a bit melodramatic. Opportunities for physical martyrdom in our line of duty are pretty rare. Nevertheless, our lives abound with innumerable, small intimations of death—in the waxing and waning of relationships, in the things that we must give up, in the hopes we must let go. In administration, as my former boss once told me, "you die a thousand deaths for the good of the whole."

Among the deaths that administrators are called to endure are many of the lessons that have been addressed in previous chapters. For example, in the acquisition of humility, administrators inevitably experience a death of the ego as they come to a new awareness of their own shortcomings and limitations. In learning trust, the need to control must die, allowing one to realize that the institution served has a life of its own in which administrators can participate, but never completely manage. The chaos will never be mastered. In becoming generative, administrators often confront—ironically—the death of productivity, wherein they must give up something else that they had hoped to accomplish in order to deal with any one of a hundred mundane crises. The big idea they long to have never emerges. The book outlined in the back of their mind takes six years to write. Much of the ministry of administration, it turns out, is in the interruption.

If we have already talked about these things earlier, why is it important to draw attention anew to the dynamic of dying in each of these administrative growth opportunities? It's essential because the image of death and resurrection is absolutely central to any discussion of a Christian spirituality. At the heart of the Christian faith is the proclamation, "Christ has died. Christ is risen." Jesus, the one we claim to pattern our lives after, consciously walked into suffering and death on the Cross—eyes wide open—and on the third day, he emerged from the tomb. When we go into the baptismal font desiring to become his disciples, we are baptized into Christ's death as we go into the water and share in his rising as we emerge on the other side. This Baptism, however, is not only an end but also a beginning. It lets us know that we can expect that our entire lives will henceforth be imprinted with this pattern of dying and rising.

Indeed, every Christian vocation, if it is a true vocation, will bear the markings of this paschal mystery. It is by experiencing the paschal mystery in our own lives that we are saved—in essence, that we are brought into the fullness of life that God dreams for us. Far from being an indicator that it is not one's call, the grace to suffer and die small deaths along the journey of a particular vocation is often the clearest sign that one is on the right vocational path. Deborah Humphreys, S.C., in writing about vocation, notes: "You did not choose this; it chose you. If you had refused, you would have other regrets. Take your chances." There is no way around suffering and death as a Christian; there are only ways through.

With that said, it seems important to make a distinction between suffering that is purposeless—against the will of God—and suffering that is paschal or transformative. Sometimes it can be hard to tell the difference between the two. God never desires suffering for its own sake, and those who deliberately create or seek suffering for themselves take a detour from the essential Christian path. As long ago as the thirteenth century, St. Angela Foligno had already noted, "Penances voluntarily undertaken are not half so meritorious as those imposed on us by the circumstances of our lives and cheerfully born." We never need to intentionally add suffering to the mix of our lives for the sake of becoming a better person. Indeed, we are to avoid unnecessary suffering because suffering has the capacity to deform and stunt and is dangerous. But the reality is that life naturally hands us any number of sufferings that we can't avoid, and in that case, the question shifts to one of response.

One possible image to help distinguish unnecessary, unholy suffering from paschal suffering comes to us in the book of Exodus, chapter 3. Moses is pasturing his sheep in the desert when he comes upon a bush on fire. There would be nothing particularly unusual about a bush on fire in such a dry area. What is unusual, and hence draws Moses's eye, is that this bush is burning but is not consumed.

There is a kind of suffering that consumes persons and leaves them feeling used up, as if a heap of ash. And then there is a kind of suffering that purifies and ignites persons, making them more translucent, bearers of light. God speaks through the bush that burns but is not consumed.

Perhaps in the end it is not that the fire is so different, but that the mystery of grace works within the person to respond to the fire in a different way. If administration, or any other vocational path, regularly leaves you feeling like a heap of ash by the end of the day, then this probably *is* a sign to do some discernment about God's call in your life. God's will for us is joy, not misery. But if administration, or any other vocational path, makes you glow even as it singes—if you are slowly becoming a holier person in the context of your work, even if it doesn't feel like it on any particular given day—then the death you are experiencing can properly be called paschal. And it is integral to one's Christian discipleship to remain *aflame*, uncomfortable though it may be.

In her book *Carnal Acts*, Nancy Mairs, a writer and teacher who lives with multiple sclerosis, describes well what it means to live aflame:

> To view your life as blessed does not require you to deny your pain. It simply demands a more complicated vision, one in which a condition or event is not either good or bad but is, rather, good and bad, not sequentially but simultaneously. Fear and anger and grief feel so unpleasant to us that we're eager to transform them into confidence and affection and joy but you can't transform what you haven't grasped . . . and so I say, "Where will it all

> end? I'm afraid." But I don't give into my fears. . . . By speaking my fear aloud, I've reduced it from a giant trampling my interior landscape to an ordinary imp, the kind who dances thru everybody's inner house from time to time, curdling the milk and smashing the crockery but leaving the structure basically intact. Surveying the damage, I get out my mop and broom. "This is my life," I say to myself, "fear and all. I'm responsible for it. And I'd better get on with it because it matters."

When we learn to embrace the recurring small (and sometimes quite large!) deaths that our vocational journey presents—when we learn to keep Mairs's "mop and broom" always handy—then we find that we have been preparing unwittingly for that one final human death that our whole lives anticipate. For if we have learned to welcome death repeatedly along the way, when we arrive at our final moment, we will know what to do because we have practiced so many times before. We will throw ourselves once more into the hands of the living God and know that, whatever happens, we will not be consumed. In the end, every vocational journey is mere preparation for that final fling of faith.

Companion for the Journey: **Rose Philippine Duchesne**

Feast: **November 18**

It might be called the curse of the administrator: the constant complaint of too much to do—the desire to be relieved of just a few of one's innumerable duties so as to have some time for quiet and reflection. But then, as soon as opportunities for quiet and reflection are afforded, we feel that restless urge to do something, to take on yet one more project. Rose Philippine Duchesne suffered this curse much of her life.

"I am very tired of my worldly life. I long for the day when we can secure our own little convent and I shall see no more of the streets," she wrote as a young sister. Yet, she confesses a short time later, "See how I reach out to many activities when I have not even a firm foothold yet; but desires are unruly when one realizes what needs there are." "I love the solitude, and I would love it even more had I more of it," she wrote to the bishop in her old age. But a letter to her cousin reads, "It seems I have outlived myself. I see the time coming when I shall be good for almost nothing. . . . That uselessness will be harder to bear after I have had so much to do."

Rose Philippine Duchesne was a woman who consistently wished she could have two lives at the same time. In her struggle to merge them into the one she was given, she models well what it means to embrace death as an administrator.

Philippine was born on August 29, 1769, in Grenoble, France. While she was still young, her family sent her to Ste-Marie-d'en-Haut monastery near her home to be educated. Loving the regulated structure of convent life, she entered the community in her teens, but she was forced to leave when the monastery closed during the French Revolution. For twelve years, she experimented with living a contemplative life on her own, while simultaneously harboring dreams of going across the ocean to serve Native Americans.

As soon as the political situation permitted it, Philippine used her family's income to lease the old Visitation monastery. She wanted to re-create the happy days that she had known there, inviting back the former nuns with whom she had lived. Few, however, returned, and those who did quickly left, complaining Philippine had created too demanding a structure. Only Philippine and two other women remained, with a few student borders.

At that point, fortuitously, Philippine met Fr. Joseph Varin, who alongside Madeleine Sophie Barat and her brother, Louis, was in the process of creating a new religious congregation of women dedicated to blending active teaching ministry with a contemplative lifestyle. Philippine and Sophie joined forces, making Ste-Marie-d'en-Haut into the second foundation of this new congregation, eventually called the Society of the Sacred Heart of Jesus.

Sophie stayed at Ste-Marie for a year, initiating Philippine and the others into the spirituality of the new congregation. Although she was a decade younger than Philippine, she was a woman of great spiritual maturity who helped Philippine address the scrupulous tendencies that had contributed to her earlier challenges to knit together a religious community. Sophie emphasized that a life of contemplation and service was possible, but it required balance and flexibility on Philippine's part.

When Sophie Barat left Ste-Marie to found other houses of the new congregation, Philippine was entrusted with multiple administrative duties: secretary to the superior, head of the boarding school, and business manager of the school and the convent. With her propensity for structure channeled toward the organizational needs of the community, Ste-Marie's flourished. In 1815, Philippine was asked to serve as Sophie Barat's secretary and treasurer for the society, roles that she fulfilled most ably. Indeed, when Philippine began to pester Sophie about being missioned to the Americas, Sophie initially declined the request, unwilling to let such a highly capable assistant go. Yet, Sophie's brother, Fr. Louis Barat—an acquaintance of Bishop William DuBourg—took Philippine's side and persuaded his sister to send a small band of the Society of the Sacred Heart to teach in the bishop's new Louisiana diocese. The diocese—essentially the whole of Thomas Jefferson's Louisiana Purchase, from the Mississippi River to the Rocky Mountains—was vast, with few cities, little infrastructure, and no schools or hospitals.

Philippine Duchesne, now forty-eight years old, and four other sisters departed on February 8, 1818, for St. Louis, Missouri, the emerging city that Bishop DuBourg had envisioned as the hub of his immense territory. The journey across the Atlantic took seventy days, followed by an additional forty days to travel up the Mississippi River from New Orleans. Upon arrival in St. Louis, however, the bishop had changed his mind and decided that the sisters would found a school in St. Charles, a tiny rural community twenty miles outside the city. Furthermore, they would not be working with Indian children but with the children of French and English traders.

Philippine was deeply disappointed and frustrated, but it was not as if the small band could turn around. In no time, the sisters opened a boarding school, a day school, and a free school for those who could not pay tuition. It was intended that the boarding and day schools would provide enough fees for the sisters' personal needs and the needs of the free school. Unfortunately, the only school that thrived was the free school. It was a story that was to be repeated innumerable times over the next twenty years.

Although Philippine had been regarded as an able administrator and business manager in France, she was never able to successfully transfer her skills to this new setting. She had difficulty understanding the American culture and language. She was never able to master English and had few of the social graces helpful in relating to parents and donors. Furthermore, despite Sophie Barat's efforts to moderate Philippine's scrupulosity, Philippine remained almost obsessive about following rules—a significant challenge in a frontier setting. She wanted every aspect of the Sacred Heart schools in America—the schedule, the uniform, the curriculum—to reflect that of the Sacred Heart schools in France. External factors, however, also contributed to Philippine's struggles. Bishop DuBourg frequently mismanaged the small congregation's funds, forcing them into debts that they could not pay off, while moving them around at will and expecting unquestioned obedience.

The success of the new Sacred Heart boarding schools launched further south in the Louisiana territory made the struggles of the schools Philippine oversaw appear starker by contrast. Although technically Philippine was Sophie Barat's appointed superior for all of the work of the congregation in the Louisiana territory, the leadership in the other schools began to write Sophie directly, circumventing Philippine. Eventually, Sophie felt compelled to remove Philippine from general leadership of the Society in the Louisiana territory, and then from direct oversight of the St. Louis schools as well.

We can imagine that the decision to demote Philippine was very hard on both Sophie and Philippine. The two had been close friends for many years. Sophie knew that Philippine embodied the spirit of the congregation and its emphasis on service to the poor better than anyone else. But the leadership needs of the Society in the Louisiana territory had surpassed Philippine's capabilities. Sophie likely felt somewhat responsible for putting Philippine in a position she had begged from the beginning not to possess. Philippine, in return, feared that she had let Sophie down.

The friendship between Philippine Duchesne and Sophie Barat was strained in their later years as Philippine's letters often went unanswered. Sophie's administrative workload overseeing a growing international congregation surely made it difficult to keep up personal correspondence, but likely she was also unable to figure out what to say to Philippine given all the difficult decisions that had been made. Toward the end of Philippine's life there was a four-year period in which she did not receive any letters from Sophie, and the silence pained her very deeply.

It was only in Philippine's "failure" and letting go of all her attachments to particular places, plans, and persons, however, that she was able in some small, unexpected ways to finally realize a reconciliation between her two great impulses—the missionary impulse to work among the Native Americans and the contemplative impulse to have more time to pray. In 1841, Philippine was one of four Society members chosen to start a school with the Jesuits among the Potawatomi in Sugar Creek, Kansas. Initially, Philippine had not been among the select group. She was seventy-one at the time and in poor health, but the Jesuits insisted she be included. "Even if she can only use one leg, she will come," one advocate argued. "She may not be able to do much work, but she will assure success to the mission by praying for us."

The advocate's words proved an accurate description of Philippine's year at Sugar Creek. Philippine's health deteriorated quickly, preventing physical work, and Potawatomi proved an even more difficult language than English. Philippine spent long hours just sitting and praying. The Potawatomi called her *Quah-kah-ka-num-ad*, "woman who prays always." And they loved her for this, frequently bringing her fresh eggs and vegetables. Philippine discovered that even if *she* felt useless, the Potawatomi people did not feel she was. Perhaps for the first time in her life, Philippine found peace in just "being."

Philippine was able to remain in Kansas only one year before her congregation insisted upon her return to St. Charles. For the next decade, she suffered a slow decline in health, gradually losing her eyesight and her memory. Philippine spent long hours under a pear tree on the St. Charles campus, praying and conversing with the school children. She died on November 18, 1852, at the age of eighty-three.

Because Philippine Duchesne lived fairly recently, and because her correspondence has been preserved so well by the Society, we are able to know more of her real, complex story than we are of saints from more distant times. We can see how God did great things through a person who endured the same sorts of financial shortcomings, cultural challenges, and internal difficulties that we find in our institutions. Furthermore, God did great things in a person who struggled with a lot of the same conflicting impulses and limited capacities from which we suffer. We can be consoled by her quirks and foibles at the same time that we are edified by her immense strength of spirit and goodwill. Philippine Duchesne was forced to die over and over again in her ministry—not in the dramatic ways that make new headlines, but in the closing of beloved schools, in the tension that existed in treasured relationships, in the inability to realize cherished dreams. She was not the successful administrator she wanted to be for the schools she founded, but she was still a holy administrator. In the end, it is not our failures that God sees, but the quality of love behind them.

For **Reflection** *and* **Prayer**

1. What are some of the small deaths you have experienced as an administrator? Have they taught you anything about the act of dying?
2. Can you tell the story of a time when you were able to graciously let go of something very significant to you personally in the course of your work? How did this feel? What happened to you in the process?
3. How do you distinguish in your life between suffering that it seems wise to walk away from and suffering that it seems important to walk toward?
4. Is there a situation in your administrative ministry at present where you think God may be inviting you to embrace dying?

5. **How does the life of St. Rose Philippine Duchesne speak to your own struggles to let go in your ministry?**

O God of Jesus Christ,
You have revealed to us that all of life is marked by the sign of the Cross.
All of life is a journey from less to more, from death to new life.
As I go about the work of administration,
illumine for me the ways in which this paschal pattern
permeates every aspect of my ministry.
Help me to discern those areas of my job in which I need to fight and resist and hold firm from those areas where I am called to let go and die.
Help me to tell the difference between suffering I should avoid
and suffering I should embrace in fidelity to the vocation you have chosen for me.
I ask this in the name of your Son, Jesus,
who walked boldly into the death to which he was called,
knowing that whatever happened,
you were waiting on the other side of the surrender.
Amen.

Administration calls us to . . .

12. Hope

We know that all creation is groaning in labor pains even until now;
and not only that, but we ourselves, who have the first fruits of the Spirit,
we also groan within ourselves.
For in hope we were saved. Now hope that sees for itself is not hope.
For who hopes for what one sees?
But if we hope for what we do not see,
we wait with endurance.

—Romans 8:22–25

In Christianity, death never has the last word, does it? The proclamation of Christ's crucifixion never stands alone. It is always followed by the announcement of the Resurrection and the promise that Christ will come again. Christians are defined as a people of hope.

Indeed, this is the mystery we celebrate in a particular way at the close of each liturgical year and the start of the next: our firm hope that the transformation that has taken place in Christ's resurrection will take place in us and in all creation. We carry a firm hope that there will come a day when every tear shall be wiped away, when the sheep will be separated from the goats and the wheat from the chaff, when the lame will walk and the blind see, when the wolf and the lamb will lie down together, when "God will be all in all." This is our firm hope in what scripture calls the *Parousia*.

The mystery of Parousia is embedded in the core of every institution. Whether nonprofit or for profit, ecclesial or secular, the reason why any institution exists—if it is a healthy institution—is the belief that the world could be a better place than it is, and that through harnessing the members' efforts as a group, that institution can help make it so. In fits and starts, dribs and drabs, we limp along together with that dream ever before us. This strange burning ember of hope is planted deep inside every human heart and simply can't be extinguished, but at the same time it is very difficult to define.

What is hope? We use the word frequently in casual conversation. "Boy, I hope she gets that job." "I hope we get the grant." "I hope he recovers soon." "I hope the mail carrier comes bearing good news today." And yet, hope is never really located within particular things. If our wishes are not realized, hope remains. We simply hope something different. This tells us that hope is deeper than desire for a specific object or outcome. It is a mysterious strength that keeps us longing for the good, even when our desires don't come true. It keeps us struggling for the good, even when the facts look grim. Brazilian theologian Leonardo Boff describes hope as "that little flicker of fire burning at the bottom of the woodpile. More rubbish is piled on, rain puts out the flame, wind blows the smoke away. But underneath everything, a brand still burns on, unquenchable."

Some of the greatest witnesses to Christian hope that I have known are administrators—perhaps because time after time administration has placed them in such difficult situations! I think of the first principal for whom I ever worked, the champion of an underdog elementary school in Guam. In my first five months at the school, five typhoons whipped through the island. Just as she would get the roof back onto the cafeteria, off the gym roof would fly. And yet, there she was the morning after each storm with her hammer and her checklist in hand. Or, I consider the director of pastoral care at a hospital that has been part of three system mergers in less than a decade, and his having to explain anew each time why his department should continue to exist at all. Despite new computer programs, new charting procedures, and new values statements hanging on the wall, he has the same steady drive to make sure the patients receive the best, even with less. The stories could go on and on. Hope reigns.

In watching administrators such as these at work, I've come to think about the virtue of hope as an amplifier for all the other qualities described in this book. Hope takes a spiritual fruit or habit and magnifies its effects, bumping it to the next level.

For example, consider what happens when hope engages the qualities of trust and breadth of vision that we discussed earlier. Ultimately, the holistic vision that God has of and for the world—the one with which we sympathize as administrators—is so magnificent that, no matter how broad our own vision is able to become on the job, we will still fail to grasp God's vision. As administrators, we might feel we have a sense of what God dreams for the planet and—on a smaller scale—our own institutions, but how God works out these dreams will likely be in ways as entirely unexpected for us as the Resurrection was for the first disciples. Hope nudges us toward an ever-greater trust while participating in God's plan. When we find ourselves walking paths that seem utterly foreign to the designs of God, hope sustains us on the journey long enough to get to that point where we can suddenly wake up and discover, "Oh, *this* is how God is acting." As the

Dominican philosopher Ralph Powell would repeatedly say, "It is hard to see the whole picture when you are inside the frame."

Perhaps the scripture passage that illumines this point best is the familiar Lukan story of Emmaus, in which two disciples are walking together on the road away from Jerusalem. They are discussing the death of Jesus and how this event has dashed the many hopes that his ministry had birthed in their hearts. Jesus walks up alongside them, but they cannot recognize him in his Parousia body. After listening to their version of the story, he begins to reinterpret the events for them so that they can see the crucifixion in an entirely new light. As it turns out, that for which they longed is still in the process of realization, but God's way of bringing it about is even more brilliant than what they had imagined. Hope has made it possible for their trust and vision to expand exponentially.

A few summers ago, I had the privilege of staying at the motherhouse of the Immaculate Heart of Mary sisters as their community president, Mary Frances Gilleran, was dying. Gilleran was one of their younger members, a woman of great creativity and vivacity whom they had elected with the expectation that she would be able to bring these gifts to bear in planning for the future of their community. Unfortunately, not long after she was elected, she was diagnosed with cancer. In the weeks before her death, she took advantage of the opportunity to plan her own memorial service and funeral, crafting the message she wanted to leave with her sisters. She wrote:

> That very same day, a group of them were on their way into a common future, which lay just ahead, beyond what they could see. As they lived into the future, they talked together about all the happenings among them. As they talked and discussed with one another, God joined them and moved into the future in their midst. But something kept them from seeing and understanding that it was really happening that *ordinarily*.
>
> God entered their hearts and asked, "What is it you are troubled about? What are you wondering? What questions are unsettling to you?"
>
> The group stopped, full of fear and anxiety. And one among them said,
>
> "We thought it would be simpler.
>
> We thought it would be more clear.
>
> We thought that the choices would be more evident.
>
> We thought we would agree more easily on what decisions to make.
>
> We thought we knew how things would be.
>
> We thought God would lead us more directly.
>
> We thought the way would have no conflicts, doubts, or confusion.

We had hoped our future would be uncomplicated.

We had hoped things would not be so messy.

We had hoped the power to choose would be easy.

We had hoped our experiences would confirm what we knew, not change it again.

We had hoped that familiar theories would still fit.

We had hoped.

We had hoped.

And now some among us are saying that things are not as we first imagined them to be. Now some are saying that the future continues to challenge us in different ways."

And God said, "How slow you are as a group. How hard it is for you to trust. Have I not promised from the beginning to be with you, to sustain you, and to continually reveal my plans to hearts that are open? Have I not promised you more than you can ask or imagine?"

And God spent time going over the history of The People Gathered and the ways that the mystery continues to be revealed. God raised up many ordinary events and interactions and showed The People Gathered God's own way of being with the people.

By the time the people had begun to understand the depth, breadth, length and height of the

> love of God for them, they were already another step into the future.

Mary Frances Gilleran and her sisters taught me a great deal about the way hope enlarges vision and the way it stretches trust.

In my own life, I have been most aware recently of the way hope magnifies agape and generativity, taking the capacities to love and to act and permeating them with a sense of urgency. While hope is oriented toward a different sort of future, I see how it energizes the present. It motivates one to sacrifice generously and freely without counting the cost, even when one might never get to see the end results of the effort. Hope increases the desire to see the good done, even if one is never thanked. It is a tremendous motivator. Listen to the passion exude from Rubem Alves, another Brazilian theologian, when he preaches:

> Let us plant dates even though those who plant them will never eat them. We must live by the love of what we will never see. This is the secret discipline. . . . Such disciplined love is what has given prophets, revolutionaries, and saints the courage to die for the future they envisaged. They make their own bodies the seed of their highest hope.

I do not know if I model Alves's "disciplined love" well. As I mentioned at the beginning of this book, I have suffered frustrations and doubts, waves of disillusionment, and whiffs of burnout. But I also acknowledged that I am still here. And in the end, I would have to say that it is because of the discovery of hope deep inside of me that I am. Despite rubbish, rain, wind, fire, and death—lo and behold—hope is still there. I still love the dream of the Parousia, and I still like contributing to it through the organizing and maintaining ministry of administration. The ember has not been extinguished. I still want to give myself, my daily labor, and indeed my body as a "seed of my highest hope."

A few years ago, at a particularly low point in my administrative career, I had the opportunity to have breakfast with an administrator I admire a great deal, who serves in an institution similar to mine. She is a generation older than me and has made substantive contributions to the field. I am in awe of the strength that has kept her so positive and active over so many years. In the past, when I felt down, I would look at her and think, "Well, if she still finds meaning in this work then *I* surely can stay." But I desperately wanted her secret. Over a stack of pancakes that morning, I was finally able to ask her, "What gives you the greatest hope? What keeps you going?" "Well," she replied, "knowing that there is a new generation like you who are still finding energy in the ministry. When I feel discouraged, I remember you are there." I couldn't decide whether to be very flattered or very alarmed. I kept going because she kept going, but she kept going because I kept going? This seemed to be a perilously fragile arrangement for the Church of the future. But then I realized, yes, that is probably the way the ember of hope has always been fanned throughout history. Sometimes you carry me and sometimes I carry you. And together we give each other the strength to keep doing what we do.

Companion for the Journey: **Gregory the Great**

Feast: **September 3**

Being pope has not been considered an easy job in any age. But being pope during the Dark Ages? Well, any respectable candidate for the position should probably have had his head examined. Pope Gregory I certainly felt that way:

> When I was living in the monastery, I was able to restrain my tongue from idle talk and to keep my mind almost constantly intent on prayer. But after the burden of pastoral care was placed on the

> shoulders of my heart, my mind could not recollect itself, being divided among many cares. For I am compelled to deal with the affairs of churches, now of monasteries, often to judge the lives and actions of individuals. Then again, to undertake the business of some citizens, to worry about the swords of invading barbarians, to fear the wolves threatening the flock. When the mind, divided and torn, is drawn into so many and such weighty matters, when can it return to itself?

Gregory found the demands of the role overwhelming. In his writing, he often gives the impression that he would have preferred to be sitting anywhere other than on the Chair of Peter. Yet, in his fourteen years as pope, Gregory served with such tenacity and doggedness that popular lore has accorded him with the rare honor of being called "the Great"—a title associated with only one other pope in Church history.

Gregory was born around the year AD 540 to a wealthy Roman family who owned the property immediately opposite the Palatine Hill, the center of Roman antiquity. North of the family estate was the Colosseum, and to the south was the Circus Maximus. The Roman Forum was right around the corner. But in Gregory's time, all of these renowned historical sites lay in ruin. The massive empire that once encircled the entire Mediterranean had split in two during the fourth century. And while the eastern half flourished with its new capital, Constantinople, the western half suffered devastating attacks from various Germanic armies and could no longer provide safety, much less prosperity, for its people. In the absence of any viable long-term government structure, the Church had assumed more and more responsibility for the basic needs of society—becoming involved in negotiating peace treaties, promoting civil order, securing food, and seeking foreign aid.

Gregory's childhood was lived under the cloud of constant war and disease. Nevertheless, he was well educated by his parents for a career in law. As a young adult, Gregory assumed the position of city prefect, responsible for oversight of law and order in Rome. Earlier in history, this position would have been looked upon with great honor, but by the time of Gregory's arrival, the city was in such disarray that he found himself unable to effect much good. After two frustrating years, he resigned.

Gregory made the decision to leave politics and embrace the contemplative life, forming St. Andrew's monastery on his Roman estate. But his retreat from the world was short-lived because in 578 Gregory was recruited by the pope to serve as one of the seven deacons of the city. The deacon was considered the bishop's right-hand man, a role of significant administrative service. Gregory was designated as the pope's ambassador—or *apocrisiarius*—to Constantinople. For six years, Gregory represented the pope in the imperial courts. His chief task was to persuade the emperor to send greater assistance to Rome to repel increasing attacks by one of the Germanic groups known as the Lombards. In this he failed; the emperor never sent the desired assistance, and Gregory was eventually called home.

The Rome he found upon his return was in even worse shape than the Rome he had left. Waves of plague ravaged the populace. Severe flooding along the Tiber wiped out innumerable homes and farms. Even the papal grain silos—used to feed the poor and refugees—were destroyed. In 590, amid the worst of the crisis, the pope was stricken by the plague and died. By popular acclamation, Gregory was chosen to replace him.

As suggested earlier, Gregory was not keen to assume the role. Some accounts have him attempting to flee Rome in a wicker basket lifted over the city walls and hiding in the forest for three days before being discovered. Curiously, Gregory's feast day—September 3—is not the date of his death (the usual date chosen for a saint's feast), but rather the day he returned to the city and submitted to the will of the people. For Gregory, this likely was a death of sorts, but the cry of the people could not be ignored. He wrote of the incident:

> There are some who, though endowed with great gifts, flee from serving their neighbors because they burn with longing for the contemplative life. Such people are without doubt accountable for the needs of those persons they might have helped by taking public office. How shall we judge the choice of someone who might manifestly have become useful to his neighbors, but who prefers his own retreat to the service of others, when even the Only Begotten Son of the Father came forth into our midst for the benefit of the many?

Records of Gregory's papacy give witness to what it means to pour out one's life for the good of others. Gregory is the first pope for whom we have, not only a rich library of sermons and pastoral material, but also an extensive collection of administrative documents. Gregory ordered that a register be kept with a copy of all his correspondence, and 854 letters still survive. His is the first papacy in which we can track the Roman chancery's day-by-day activity. We are able to see the detailed care with which Gregory stewarded the papacy's resources, most especially its land.

During the period of Gregory's administration, scholars estimate the estates of the Church to have been somewhere in the vicinity of 1800 square miles, making Gregory one of the largest landlords in all of Europe. Conscious of the bodily needs of the human person as well as the spiritual, Gregory saw the estates as a means of helping to alleviate hunger and famine. It was important to him that they were well managed, that the tenants were treated fairly, and that the food produced was widely distributed. Gregory's correspondence gives evidence that he was deeply involved in consolidating the affairs of these estates so that they could be more fruitful. He debated the exact number of *sextarii* in a *modius* of corn, complained about the use of false weights by certain traders, and appointed honest clerics to serve as his agents in the field. There are many stories of Gregory's handing out food himself on the first of each month and of his serving the poor of Rome at his own table. Profits from the land were regularly used to pay bribes and ransoms to the Lombards in order to ensure stability and safety for the inhabitants of Rome.

Yet, Gregory's concern for his people, of course, extended beyond the physical. One of the earliest writings of his papacy was a handbook for bishops on pastoral care. It is the first of its kind in Church history—giving advice on how to counsel and offer spiritual direction. Gregory advocated for nuanced and careful discernment, recognizing that different situations called for different responses. Liturgy also received his special attention. Gregory helped to standardize the way Mass was celebrated throughout western Europe—as evidenced in the Gregorian sacramentaries—while he also encouraged the development of liturgical chant.

Looking back at Gregory's papacy today, one might question appropriate boundaries between what we would now call "church and state." Gregory was involved in all dimensions of governance—military, political, economic, religious. He was known to support the use of force against Arian Christians in an effort to convert them. He was not above financial incentives to persuade non-Christians to be baptized. Gregory himself seems to have felt uncomfortable with the breadth of his power. He wrote, "Whoever is called a 'pastor' is so heavily involved in exterior business that it is often unclear whether he performs the office of a pastor or that of an earthly potentate." Yet, it is important to remember that in Gregory's time no such boundaries existed. Gregory cared about the people of Rome and was motivated to do whatever necessary to watch out for them in the midst of a vacuum of other forms of leadership.

Gregory died on March 12, 604, at the age of sixty-four. At the time of his passing, he was riddled with gout, unable to walk. Rome was under siege yet again, and another famine gripped the land. In their desperation, the people of Rome had turned against him, critical of his leadership. He died believing that the world was coming to an end, unsure whether anything he had done had had any positive impact.

Yet, the world did not end. And with time people grew to appreciate what Gregory had tried so hard to do on their behalf. In 1298, Gregory was recognized as one of the first four Doctors of the western Church, alongside Jerome, Ambrose, and Augustine. Sustained only by hope, he had shepherded the Church through one of its darkest times.

For Reflection *and* Prayer

1. Has your experience of administration increased your capacity to hope?

2. Can you tell the story of a time when your work as an administrator required you to live by hope? Can you tell of a time when you thought you knew how the puzzle pieces of life fit together, and God surprised you with an alternative picture of reality?

3. Is there a situation in your administrative ministry at present where you could really use an infusion of hope?

4. **What insights does the life of St. Gregory offer to you about what it means to live by hope?**

Spirit of God,
Deep within me resides a spark, a strength, an unquenchable hope that will not die.
No matter how I might try to walk away and say that my work has no meaning,
that nothing ever changes, that the powerful always win,
that the world is irreparably corrupt,
inside of me a still, small voice whispers, "That is not true."
And once again a fire ignites within me that dreams of the day you promise.
I want that day with all my heart, and I recommit to working with you to bring it about. May my ministry of administration be animated by the strength called "hope."
May it be fierce and persistent in the face of challenge,
steady and tenacious in the face of change.
May it nourish, energize, and sustain me so that I might more fully serve your plan.
Amen.

Administration Call Us to Too Much

The devil came to me disguised as more,
One more good thing I could do,
Should do,
And then another,
And another.
I was seduced and misguided.
The more sapped my energy, my joy, my delight.
There was more harshness and impatience
In my voice and my presence.
And the devil grinned,
While God sighed patiently
Knowing that when I get worn down enough,
I'll come home to my true self,
To being my true self in God.

—Clarence Heller ,"More"

A year is comprised of twelve months. I know that. You know that. But what of those shadowy forces responsible for the mysterious paragraphs on our job descriptions written in invisible ink? Do they know that? Apparently not. "I like the structure of your book," said one of my colleagues. "I understand the potential of exploring one habit for each month and that you provide an even dozen. But what do you have to say to those of us who have thirteen months of work to fit into twelve?" Everywhere that I have traveled in doing workshops for administrators, I have heard that question echoed. It has been phrased in a variety of ways, but the underlying angst is always the same: how can I live in right relationship with time?

Of course, I do not know the answer to the question any better than you do. I ask it myself about five times a day. But the frequency and urgency with which I have heard the question does lead me to think that this book would be incomplete if I did not acknowledge it and pose at least a few nuggets for reflection. Administrators experience the crisis of time as a profound spiritual issue. We say that we do what we do out of a love of God and neighbor, and yet at the same time we often experience the immensity of what we are asked to do as an obstacle to our relationship with God and neighbor. How do we make peace with the mystery of time?

I have struggled with the right stewardship of time for as long as I can remember. For a good while I blamed my places of employment for the fact that I was always frazzled and late, unable to concentrate, and unavailable. They were the ones stealing time from me, placing impossible demands on me. A few years ago, however, I was granted a sabbatical to work on a writing project. For a whole year, I did not have to answer my work phone or e-mails, teach a class, run a grant, advise students, or serve on a committee. As you may already suspect, it turns out that the problem was not really my job. I was still frazzled and late, unfocused, and busy beyond belief. The problem, it turns out, is largely me. The job definitely exacerbates the situation, but it is not the root cause.

I have wondered long and hard about my propensity for busyness and over-involvement. To be fair to myself, a good part of my activity is compelled by a love of life. I don't just *like* being alive—I *love* it to the *n*th degree. I find the world a fascinating place, with so many interesting things to do and so many intriguing people to meet. And I really like thinking that it could be an even better place and that I could be part of making it so. I suspect you do, too. But in all honesty, there are also some other dynamics at play. As mentioned earlier, I can have a hard time trusting that others will do the job well, leading me to micromanage and take on projects that I shouldn't. I can have a hard time trusting that God's plan involves more people than me and that God could have other means to reach a particular end. I realize that I like to be needed; it helps me to feel important. And in American society, time is a measurement of worth. If I am very busy, it means that I must be very important. Furthermore, I can avoid doing tasks that I don't really like doing and relationships that I don't really enjoy by saying that I am too busy right now. It is one of the few acceptable excuses left in our culture.

I don't know if any of the above dynamics are also at work in your life, but it could be worth asking: "In what way does my busyness serve me?" I have learned that, in the end, we only engage in behaviors that we believe serve us in some way, even if unconsciously, even if mistakenly. If we want to make peace with the mystery of time, external changes (e.g., quitting the job, requesting a reduced workload) will not make much of a positive impact on our spiritual lives unless we first have made some internal changes—namely, becoming aware of the personal needs our busyness serves and addressing those needs. Before we negotiate with our boss or our board, we need to negotiate with ourselves, lest we find ourselves in the exact same situation, just in another place. It is only in attending to our deep, internal drives that lasting, external changes become attractive and possible.

I want to offer a few resources from our larger Judeo-Christian tradition that speak to the core human drives that often undergird our busyness and perhaps might free us to act in another way.

The first insight comes from the Rite of Baptism. Often on funeral holy cards, we will see the person's date of birth and then another date labeled as "born into eternal life" rather than "date of death." From a theological perspective, this is erroneous. As Christians, we do not enter into eternal life after we die; we enter into eternal life on the day we are baptized. When we went down into the water of the font, we died with Christ. When we came up on the other side, we rose with him. Physical death will clearly be a significant moment in the ongoing transformation of our lives toward ever-deeper configuration with Christ, but the essential transformation has already occurred. You and I are already in our eternal life. And there is no reason we should be living as if this weren't the case.

A popular Christian perception images earth as a place of ceaseless labor and heaven as a place of endless rest. There are a couple of problems with this perception. Christian doctrine tells us that, as members of the Communion of Saints, even heaven will not free us from work. We will still be active on behalf of the earth's transformation even after we die. We will still be interceding for those in need. Additionally, being on earth does not free us from the obligation to receive the gift of rest. Eternity is made up of both work and rest. If we do not learn how to practice and enjoy rest here on earth, we are going to have a hard time practicing and enjoying rest in heaven.

When I was a chaplain in training some years back, I once was sent to visit a woman in the independent living quarter of a senior living facility. The woman, in her eighties, swam every day. I was captivated by this. On the first day we met, I said, "When I get older, I plan on swimming every day." She quickly responded, "Do you swim every day now?" "No," I admitted. "Then you won't when you get older either," she replied. This woman impressed upon me that I was not suddenly going to change into another person simply because I grew older, nor—by extension—even because I crossed to the other side of the grave. We need to start practicing now who we want to be in the future.

This brings us to a second resource offered by tradition, the ancient Jewish practice of Sabbath. Christians sometimes speak of Sunday as being a day of Sabbath, but this is a profound misinterpretation of the original meaning of the day. Sunday is actually the first day of the Jewish week, an important fact for understanding the theological import of the Resurrection story. The first day is the day of light's creation in the book of Genesis. The gospel writers wanted to emphasize that Christ is the new creation—Christ is the light who conquers the darkness. For early Christians, Sunday was the day of Eucharist, a day to remember the paschal mystery. But it was still a day of work. The day of rest was the seventh day of the week, the Sabbath.

On the seventh day, Genesis tells us God capped the work of creation by creating *menuha*. In English, we translate this word as "rest," but in the original Hebrew the word has layers of rich meaning, including "tranquility," "calm," and "peace." For century upon century, Jews honored the seventh day of each week by marking it as a day of *menuha*. The earliest Christians, who were Jews, did as well. But as Christianity embedded itself in other cultures, the practice of Sabbath was lost. In order to understand Sabbath fully, we need to turn to our Jewish sisters and brothers who still practice it.

One of the most well-known modern resources for understanding Sabbath is Rabbi Abraham Heschel's book by the same title, first published in 1951. Heschel's words, though now more than sixty years old, appear prescient when addressing the crisis of time that administrators face today.

> We know what to do with space but do not know what to do about time, except to make it subservient to space. Most of us seem to labor for the sake of things of space. As a result we suffer from a deeply rooted dread of time and stand aghast when compelled to look into its face. Time to us is sarcasm, a slick treacherous monster with a jaw like a furnace incinerating every moment of our lives. Shrinking, therefore, from facing time, we escape for shelter to things of space. . . . But things of space are not fireproof; they only add fuel to the flames. . . . It is impossible for man to shirk the problem of time. The more we think the more we realize: we cannot conquer time through space. We can only master time in time. The higher goal of spiritual living is not to amass a wealth of information, but to face sacred moments.

In Heschel's understanding, observing Sabbath teaches us how to "master time in time" so as to "face" those "sacred moments." Its practice is foundational to the way the world was created by God: six days a week we work, participating in the ongoing transformation of the physical world, but on the seventh day we rest. We refrain from making any change to the physical world, refraining even from thoughts about labor. For one day, things are enjoyed for what they are, not for what they could be. We remember that, at a very core level, all is well just as it is. To resist this rhythm of work and rest is to be out of sync with God's intent for creation. "This is the task of men," Heschel continues, "to conquer space and sanctify time." Sabbath, Heschel says, is "a sanctuary in time," "holiness in time," "spirit in the form of time," "eternity uttering a day."

In all honesty, I do not know what it would look like truly to observe Sabbath as a Christian. We do not have an established set of practices around Sabbath as the Jewish community does. But it does seem to me that this very ancient concept holds some much-needed wisdom for us in our present lives. Unlike other practices that Judaism perceives as obligatory only for the Jewish people, honoring Sabbath is a practice that the Hebrew scriptures indicate is meant for all: the servants in Israelite households and even animals are expected to rest on the seventh day. For us as Christians, Sabbath practice seems to offer a way of living out our baptismal belief that we are already in eternal life and should start acting like it.

In the beginning of this book, I promised that I would not be talking about adding anything to your already-busy life. In writing this chapter, I have wondered if I am breaking my promise. Am I advocating adding, not just ten minutes a day of prayer, but actually a *whole day* of prayer to your every week? How does this solve anything at all? I prefer to look at it this way: God is inviting us to drop one workday out of our week. This isn't so that we can fill that day with other activities—laundry and sports games and volunteer service and catching up on e-mail—but rather so that we enjoy the most essential gifts of being human in this world—reading and discussing with family and friends, sleeping and eating in leisure, praying, having sex with our spouse, sitting and watching the birds . . . the traditional pastimes of the Sabbath.

These activities are constitutive of being human. If we fail to participate in them in a substantive way on a regular basis, we will have failed to live God's will for our race just as much as if we had never "filled the earth and subdued it" through our labor.

Of course, this brings us back to where we started this reflection: "How do I do this?"—albeit with a slightly different nuance. We see that it is not so much a question of how to manage our time as how to manage ourselves within time. Unlike space, time is not going to bend to our will. There is nothing we can do to speed it up or slow it down. Time is beyond our control. As Heschel reminds us, "Time belongs only to God." The challenge is instead how to conform our lives to the rhythm of time that God established in creation.

Again, I want to emphasize that I have not figured out how to do this yet. Time and I continue to have a rocky friendship at best. Below are a few steps I have found important in the effort to conform to what I perceive as God's desire for humans in time.

Calendar Assessment: Write down the ten top priorities in your life, in order of priority. Then chart your use of time over the course of a week. Where is the majority of your time going? And how does this match up with what you have said are your top ten priorities? We often discover quite a wide gulf between what we say we value and what we actually value, based on how much time we have given over to it. As you review your use of time over the past week, what could you let go of in order to focus more on your stated priorities? What can be dropped from your life entirely?

Rethink Scheduling Habits: Rather than placing an empty calendar on your desk and then filling it in as people request appointments, taking whatever time is leftover for your own priorities, start each month by blocking in your priorities first and then allowing the remaining time for appointments. For the sake of flexibility, you might include zones that you would prefer not be taken but that you could open as needed. But do not place the establishment of your schedule into the hands of others before you have blocked out what is most important to you.

Radical Self-Acceptance: One of the reasons that we overcommit is that we have a hard time saying no. We don't want to disappoint others. We want to be important. We want to be liked. We want to be valued. We want to be perceived as competent and efficient. None of these are bad things, but the work that we can do—through counseling, prayer, spiritual direction, lasting friendships, and so on—to accept and love ourselves exactly as we are will go a long way toward solving our time crises. The very real need to be loved and accepted is best met in family and friendship relationships rather than in work relationships. If we can meet these core human needs elsewhere, work will take its righteous role in our life but not consume it.

Development of Discernment Skills: The world is a place of abundance, but you and I have a limited number of years to enjoy this planet. In the words of Thomas Merton, "The spiritual life is not so much about choosing between good and evil, but discerning which particular good is meant for me." One of my friends taught me that instead of praying with one's palms facing upward—a beautiful posture of receptivity to the gifts of God—sometimes it is important to pray with one's palms facing downward, resting on one's lap—an equally beautiful posture intended to convey: "I have enough. I have everything I need. I do not need any more. Let me be thankful." There will be periods in life for new learning and new possibilities, but we do not need to pursue every opportunity made available to us. Sometimes it is okay to say, "Let me just savor for a bit."

Development of Negotiating Skills: Deciding that you will say no to certain tasks and projects in order to live your "eternal life" well will inevitably put you into conflict with others who are not accustomed to your saying no. In your effort to be a better steward of your time, you will benefit tremendously from learning the skills needed to be in difficult conversations without backing down or becoming rigid. Anyone uncomfortable with conflict will have a very tough time maintaining a balanced calendar.

Praying with One's Calendar: The task of trying to live one's "eternal life" well in contemporary American society is probably more than any of us is going to be able to manage on our own. Over and over again, we will take one step forward, and then two, three, occasionally twelve steps back. We can bring our struggles with time to God explicitly in prayer, asking for the wisdom to know how to live better within the time given to us.

In the end, we may discover that we have let go of everything we can and that our time still feels chaotic. We are still tired and still surprised by how commitments that look doable from a distance are unwieldy as their date approaches. Sometimes we may just have to admit that the crisis of time is an aspect of the paschal mystery lived in the vocation of an administrator. Our learning to accept the lack of control and sense of being pulled under may be God's way of moving through what feels like our dying to new life, God's way of showing us anew what our Baptism entails. But the fact that dying remains a part of our life should not stop us from striving to live into the resurrection.

> Let them remember there is meaning beyond absurdity. Let them be sure that every little deed counts and that we can—every one—do our share to redeem the world in spite of all absurdities and all frustrations and all disappointments. And, above all, remember that the meaning of life is to build a life as if it were a *work of art*.
>
> —Abraham Heschel
> *Moral Grandeur and Spiritual Audacity*

Conclusion

About fifteen years ago, one of my first supervisors told me I had to be very careful what I prayed for, because if I prayed for patience, how else would God cultivate patience except by putting me in situations where I would need to practice it? If I prayed for courage, how else would God nurture this capacity but by putting me in situations that would require it? And if I prayed for hope—well, just thinking about what might be entailed to grow in hope is enough to make me cross that virtue off the most-desired list! But what he said is true. God molds us and shapes us into the people that God dreams us to be by placing us in circumstances that insist we become those people. Administration is difficult work; there is no way around it. Every day it asks us to become more than we are right now. In this book I chose twelve ways in which administration has beckoned me to be "more," but obviously the list could be endless. Who knows what administration may invite us toward next?

At this point in time, my prayer life looks radically different than it did when I first started this job. I have stopped praying for particular gifts altogether, because

I realize I don't always know what exactly the best thing in any given situation would be—even for myself, much less my institution, never mind the world! All I know is that the best thing that could happen would be for the will of God to be done, because I have been successfully persuaded that in the end that *is* what will make us all happiest. But this can be tough. It is not always pretty, and it is not always pleasant. So, instead of beginning the day asking for humility or breadth of vision or trust or humor, I just say to God, "Be gentle. I want for this day whatever it is you want—but just go gentle with me."

As a child, I was taught to make such an offering to God each morning—not in those words, of course, but the idea was the same: give the stuff of each day to God. As an adult, this practice has become much richer because I am able to see more clearly how it relates to the most central prayer of our faith—the Eucharist.

Catholic theology of the Eucharist is rich and profound. There are many angles from which to consider what it is that happens when we gather around the altar table and its relation to our daily life. The perspective that has been most meaningful for me in recent years comes from French paleontologist and theologian Pierre Teilhard de Chardin. He speaks about the bread we offer as representing all the activities of our daily lives that seek to contribute to the ongoing creation of the earth—the meetings and carpools, memos and networking efforts, phone calls and visits to coworkers in need. He then speaks about the wine as representing all the passivities of our daily lives that challenge and even diminish us—the obstacles and losses, personality quirks that limit our potential, illnesses and aging. In the Eucharist we ritually bring these activities and passivities of our lives and offer them as a gift to God. We unite our lives to the life of Jesus Christ, who also offered his whole life as a gift, with a totality and freedom to which we can still only aspire. We say in essence, "God, everything I have received in this life, I received as a gift from you. This is what I've managed to do with your gifts so far. Now, I return my life to you as a gift. Take it and transform it. However messy or insane it might look, fill it with your Spirit so that somehow it contributes to your larger plan for our planet. May all the building up and tearing down going on in my life right now somehow give praise to you." Eucharist is the key that helps us decipher the map of our daily life. It helps us make sense of the terrain we walk. It helps us journey toward the place we want to go.

We began this book with a short passage from St. Paul. Perhaps it is most fitting to allow him to also have the last word, since he captures so well what it means to live all one's life as gift.

> I urge you therefore . . . by the mercies of God, to offer your spiritual worship.
>
> Since we have gifts that differ according to the grace given to us, let us exercise them: if prophecy, in proportion to the faith; if ministry, in ministering; if one is a teacher, in teaching; if one exhorts, in exhortation; if one contributes, in generosity; *if one is over others, with diligence*; if one does acts of mercy, with cheerfulness. . . . Love one another with mutual affection; anticipate one another in showing honor. Do not grow slack in zeal, be fervent in spirit, serve the Lord. Rejoice in hope, endure in affliction, persevere in prayer.
>
> Do not be conquered by evil but conquer evil with good.
>
> —Romans 12:1,6–8; 10–12; 21
> (emphasis mine)

Would you pray that God might help me to embody Paul's challenge today in my administrative tasks? That my work might be holy and pleasing? That whatever I am called to do today, I'll do it with diligence? And know that I will be praying for you. Together let us make administration our spiritual worship.

Ann M. Garrido has been a member of the faculty at Aquinas Institute of Theology in St. Louis since 1999. In addition to teaching, she has served the school in a variety of administrative capacities, including program director for the doctor of ministry in preaching, director of the master's in pastoral studies and Catechesis of the Good Shepherd, director of field education, director of distance learning, and director of the Aquinas Ministry Integration Project. Most recently, she oversaw a three-year grant project that established new best practices for conflict management. She is the author of *Mustard Seed Preaching* and *A Concise Guide to Supervising a Ministry Student* and also serves as senior editor of *Human Development*.

Founded in 1865, Ave Maria Press, a ministry of the Congregation of Holy Cross, is a Catholic publishing company that serves the spiritual and formative needs of the Church and its schools, institutions, and ministers; Christian individuals and families; and others seeking spiritual nourishment.

For a complete listing of titles from

Ave Maria Press

Sorin Books

Forest of Peace

Christian Classics

visit www.avemariapress.com